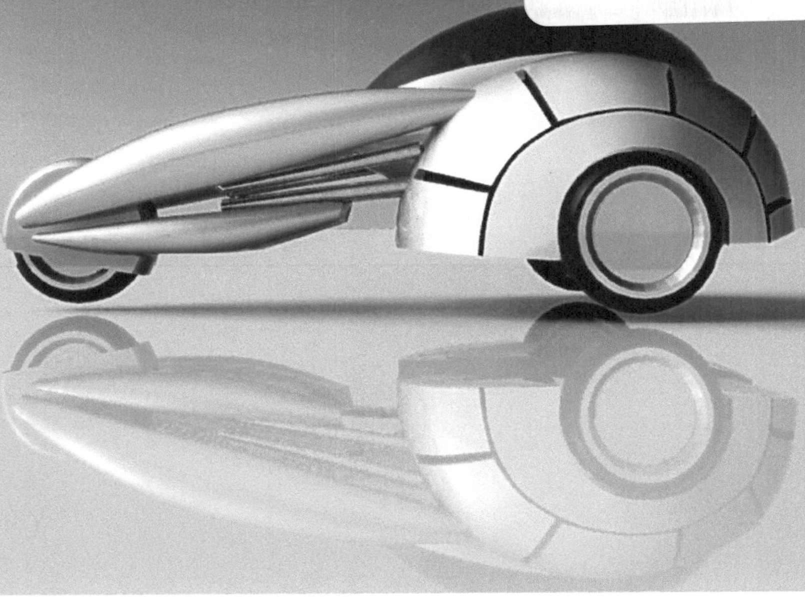

SUN CHARIOTS PROJECT
MARCO AURELIO GALAN HENRIQUEZ

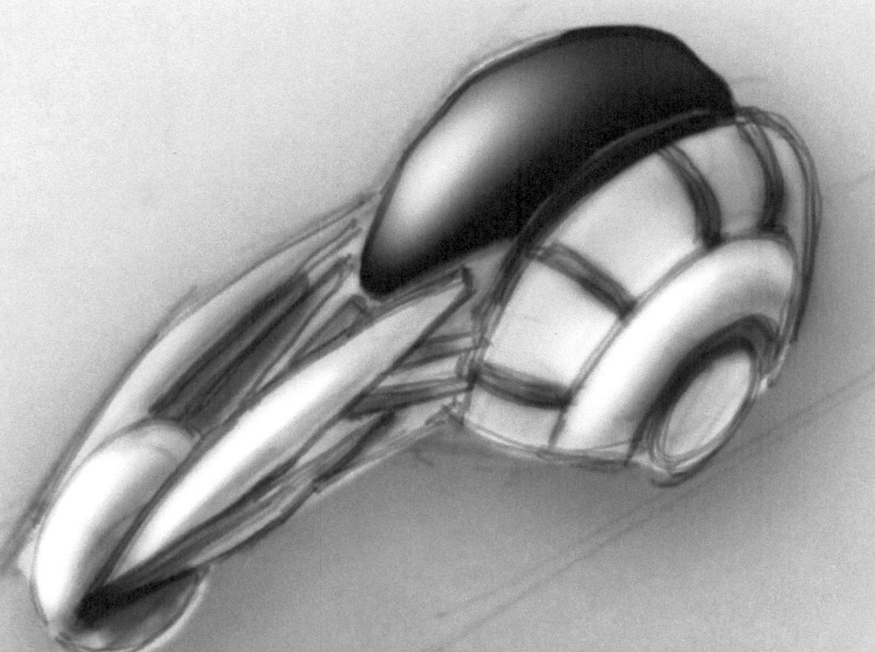

CONTENTS

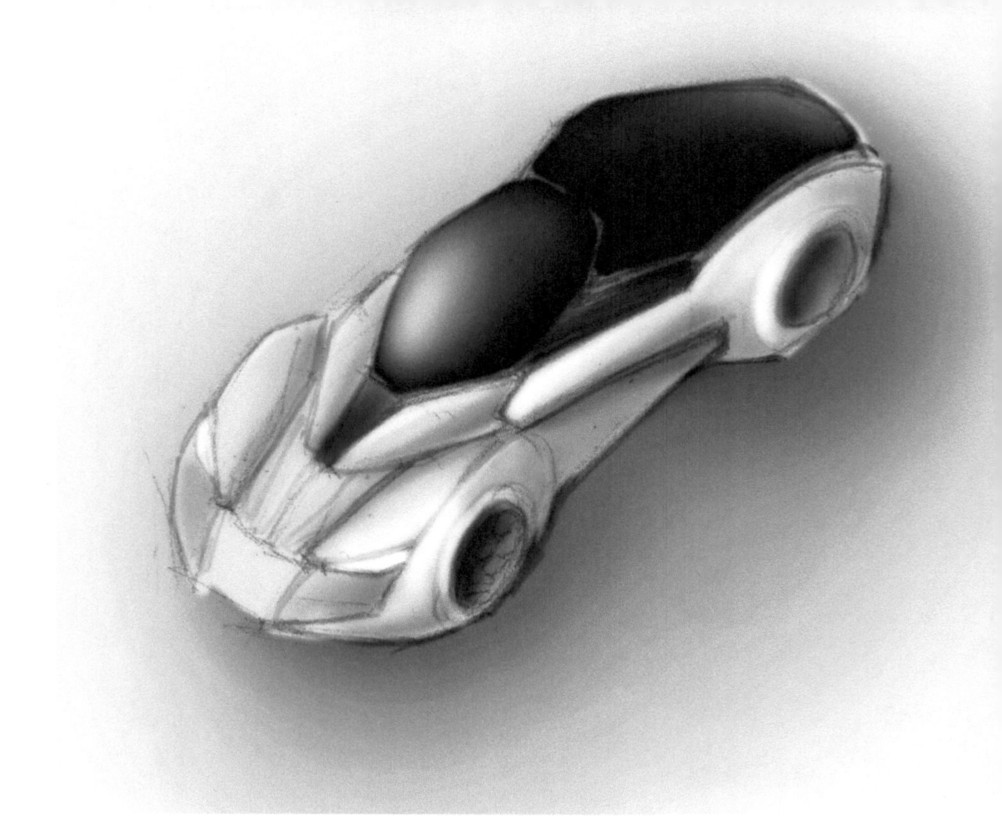

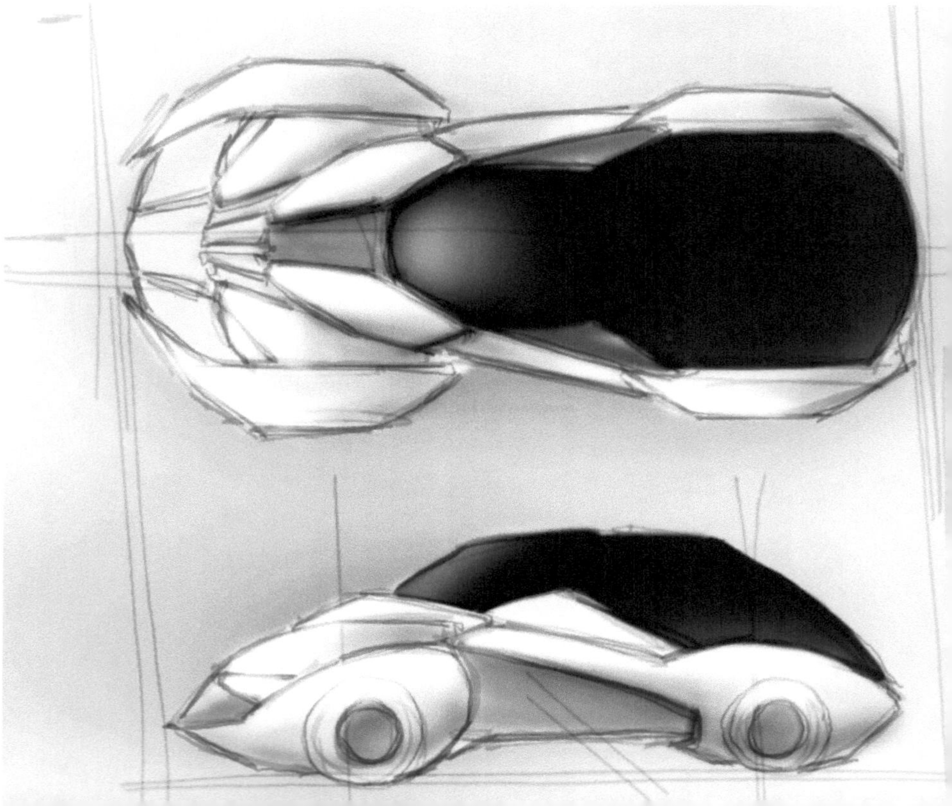

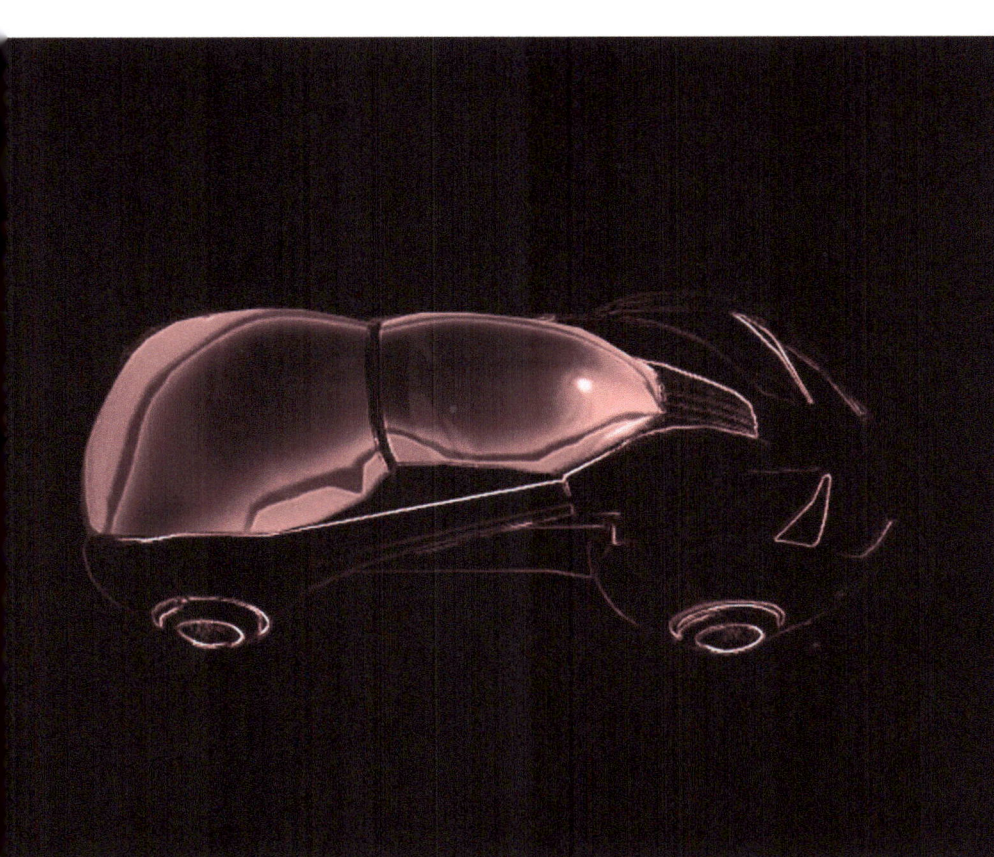

ASTAROTH

3

4

6

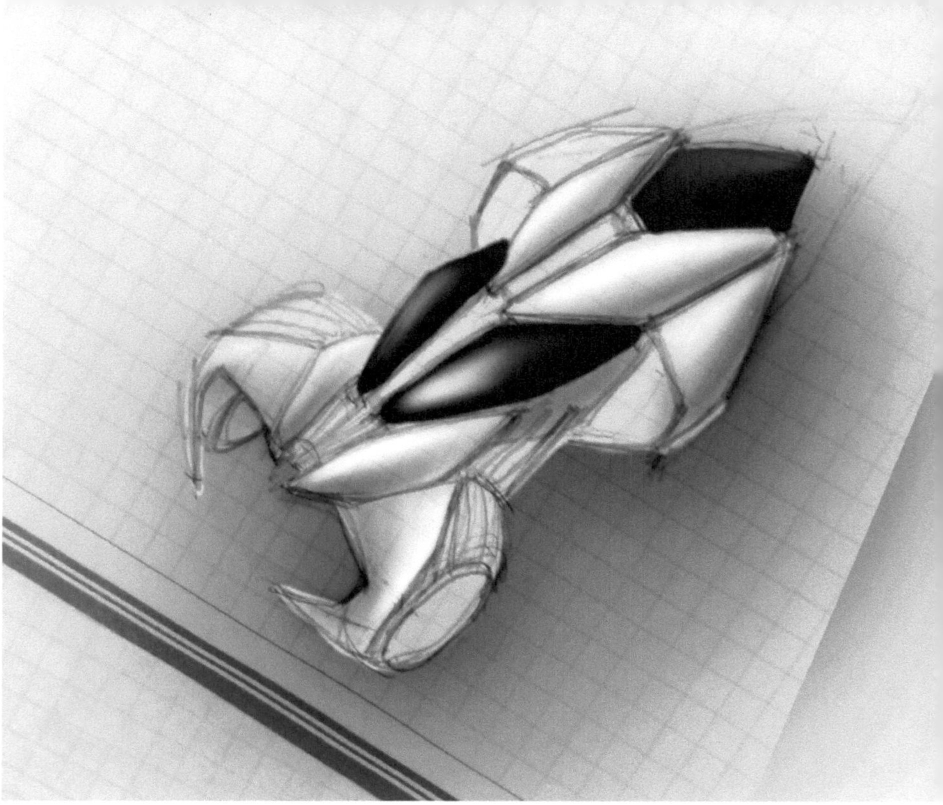

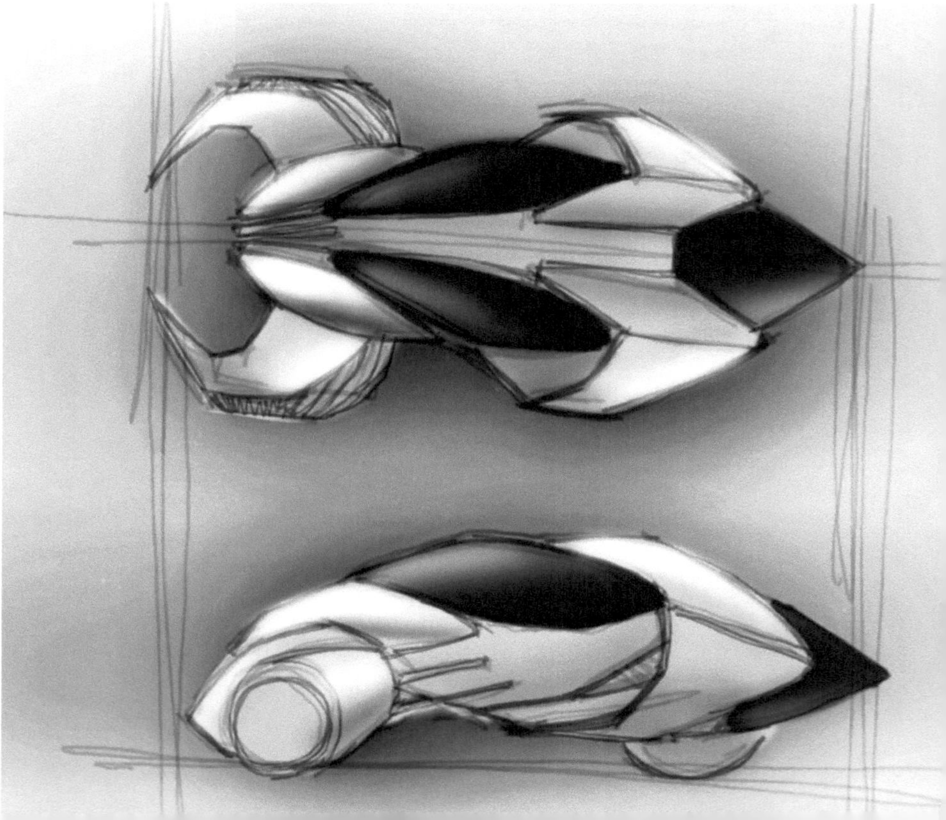

ANDRAS

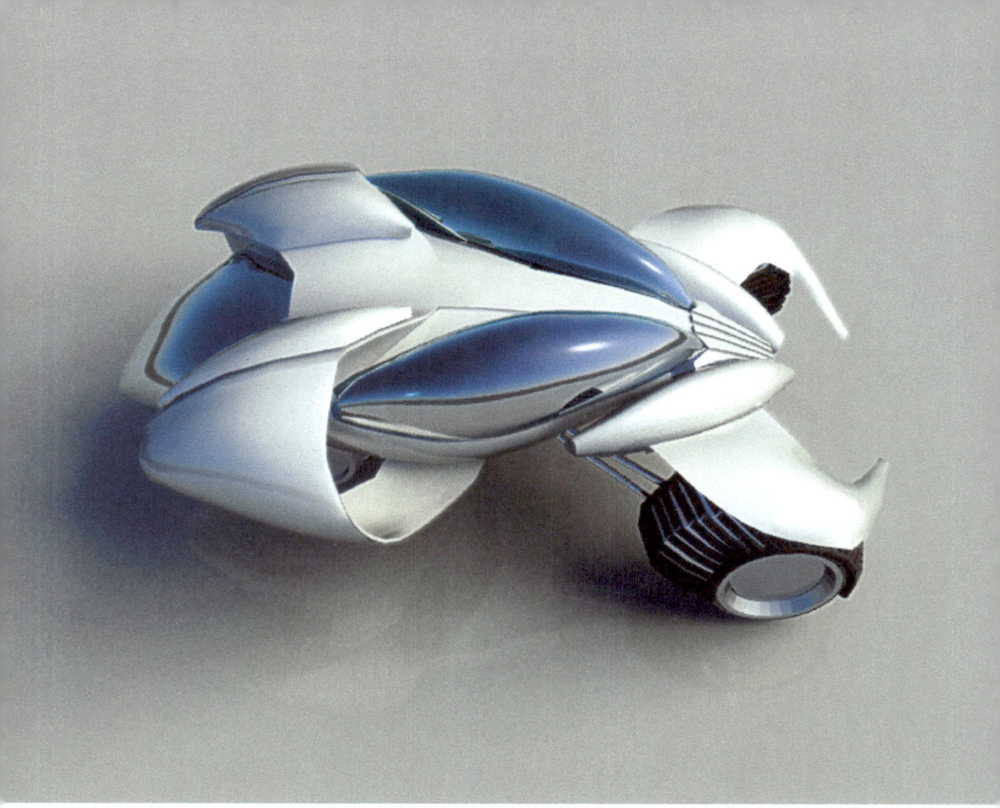

9

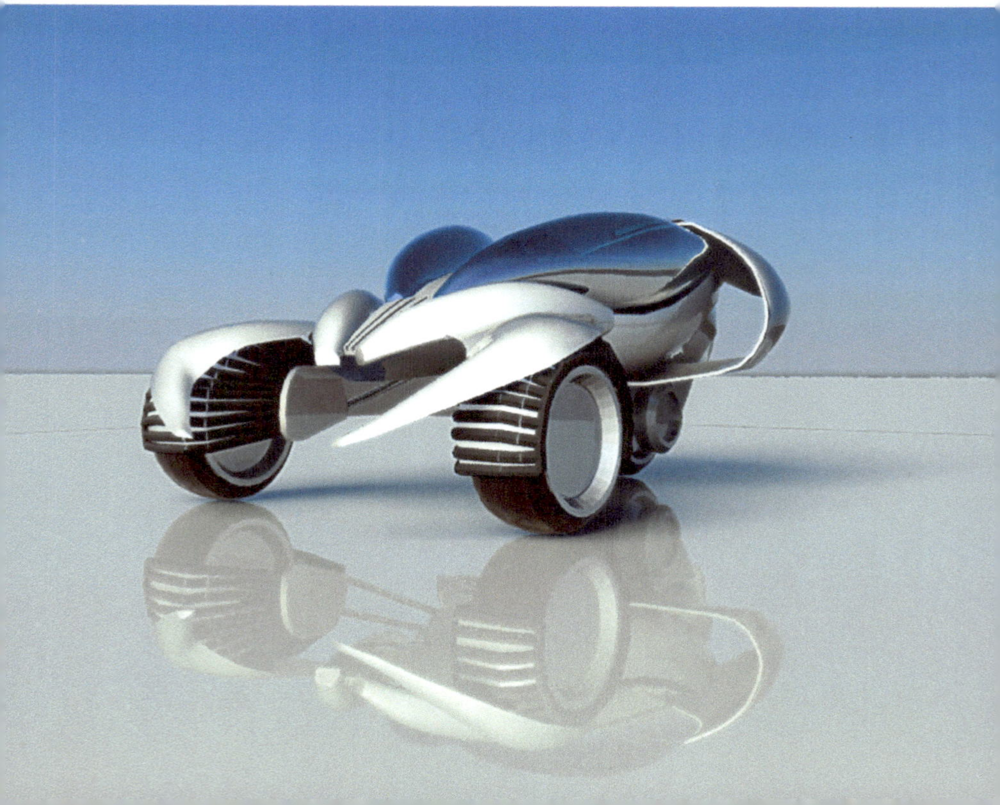

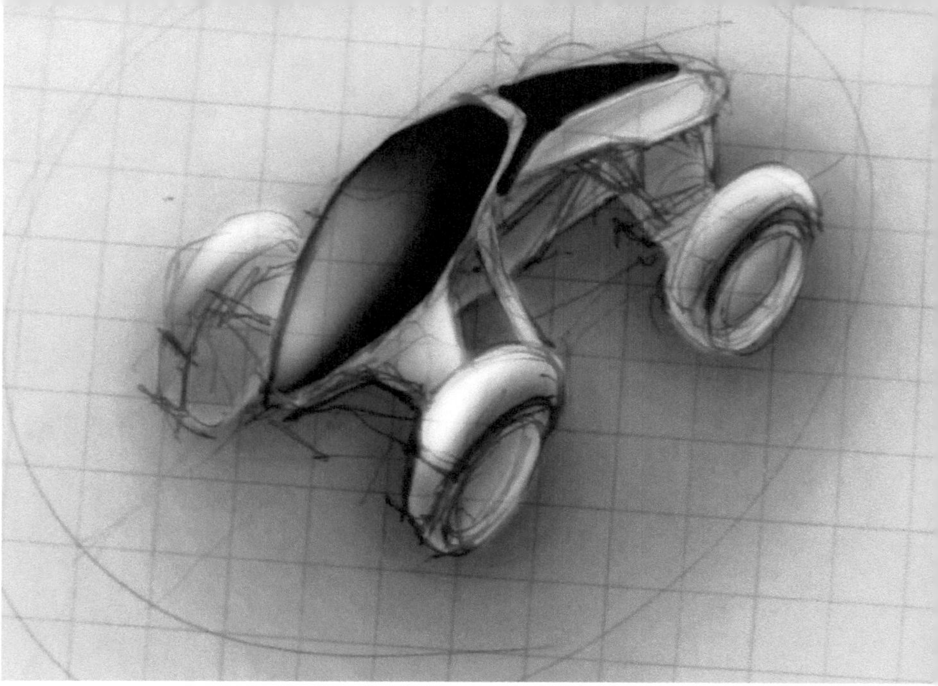

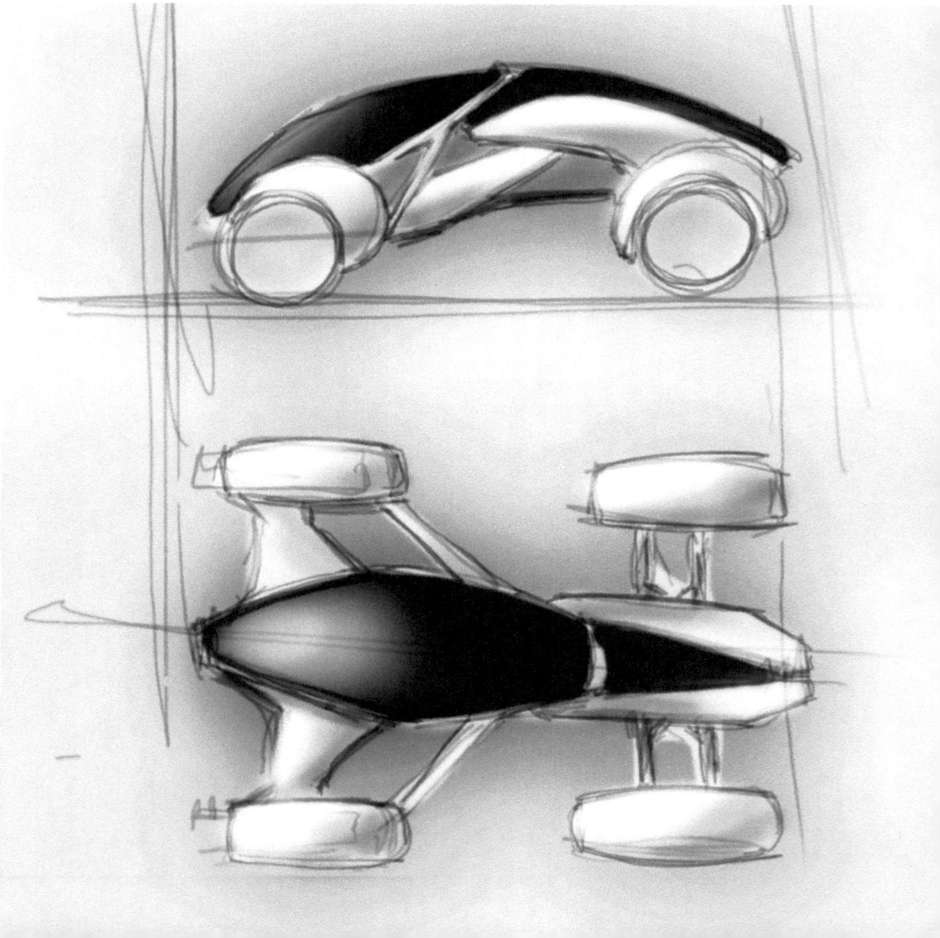

HALPHAS

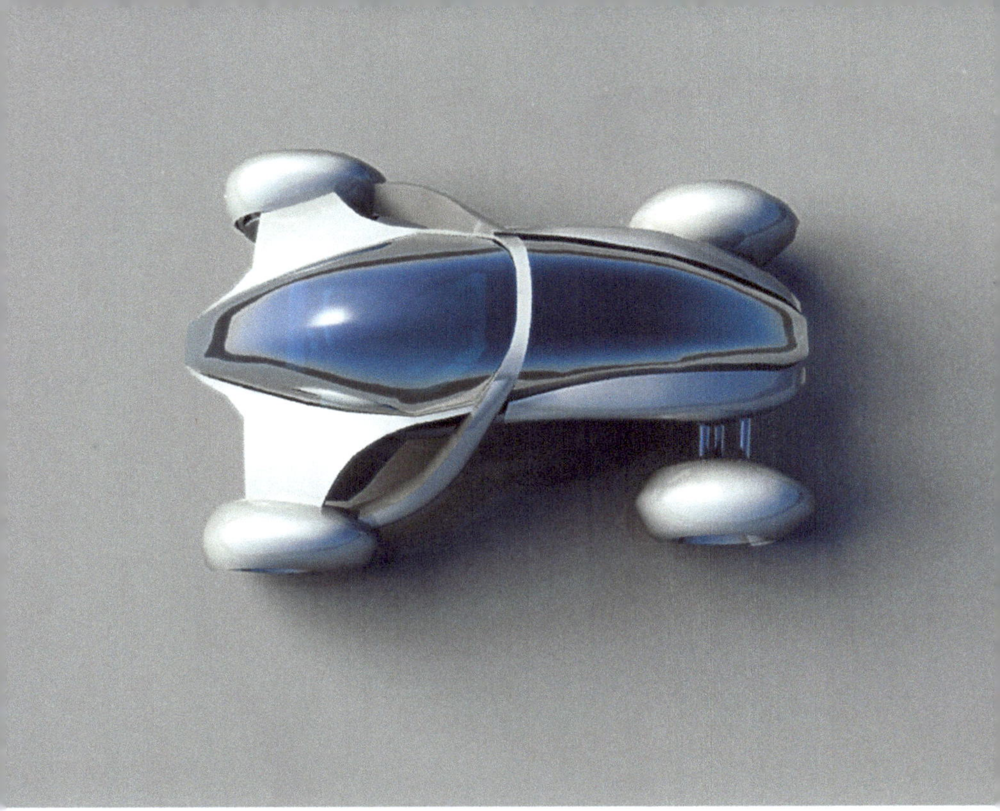

18

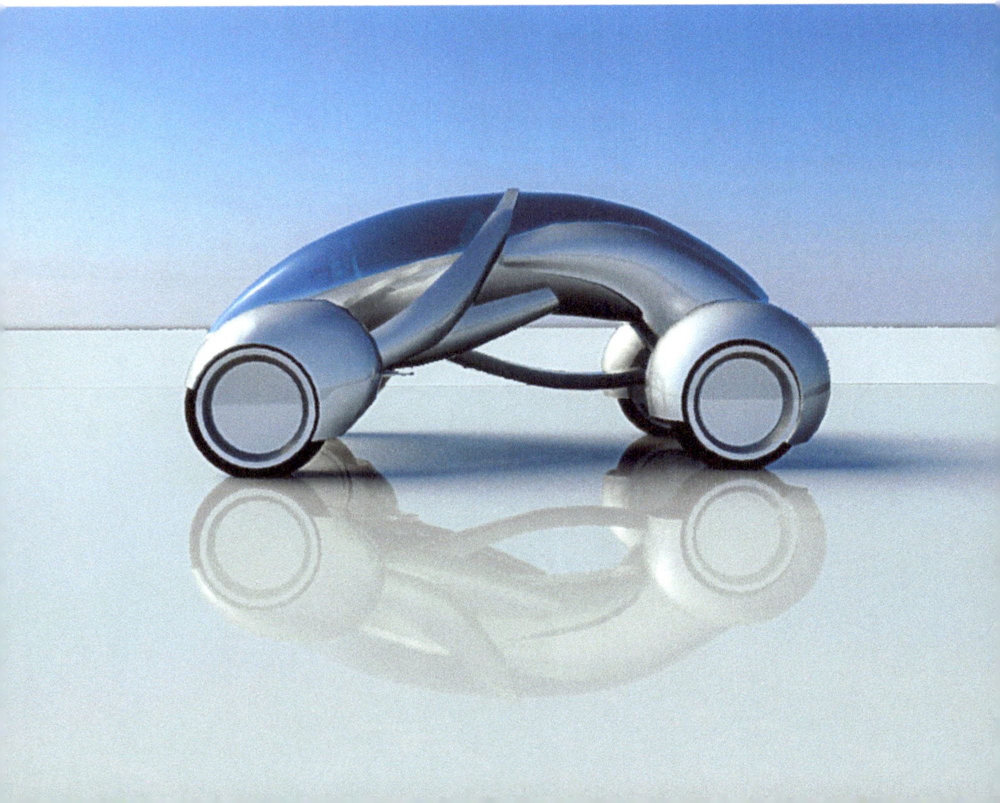

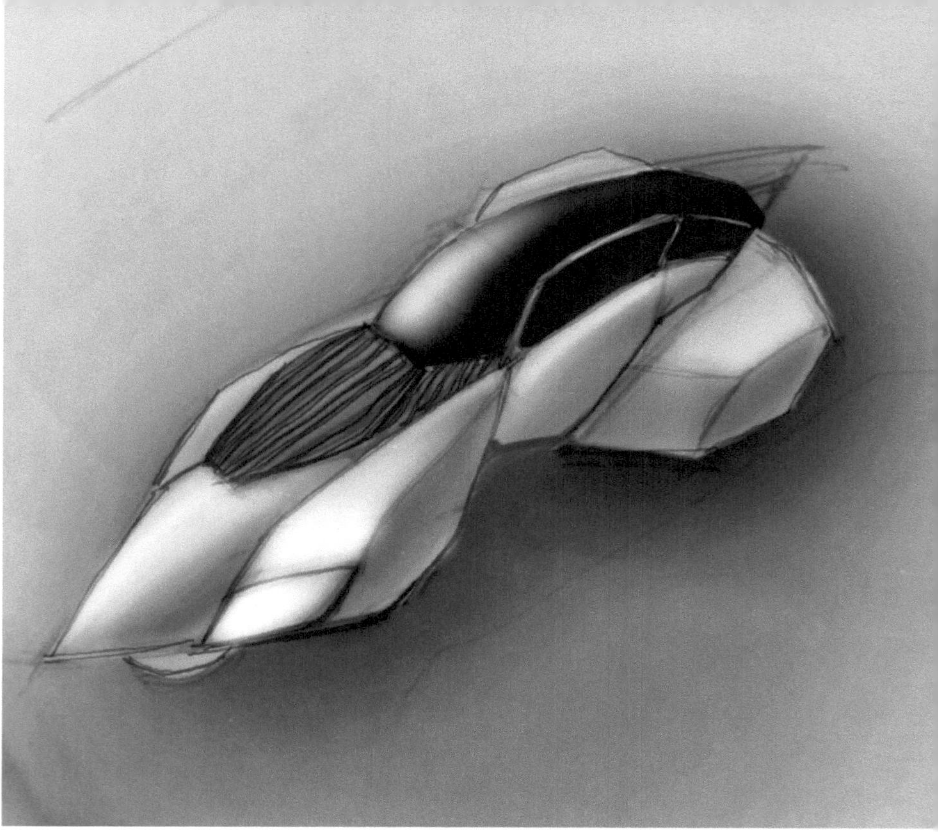

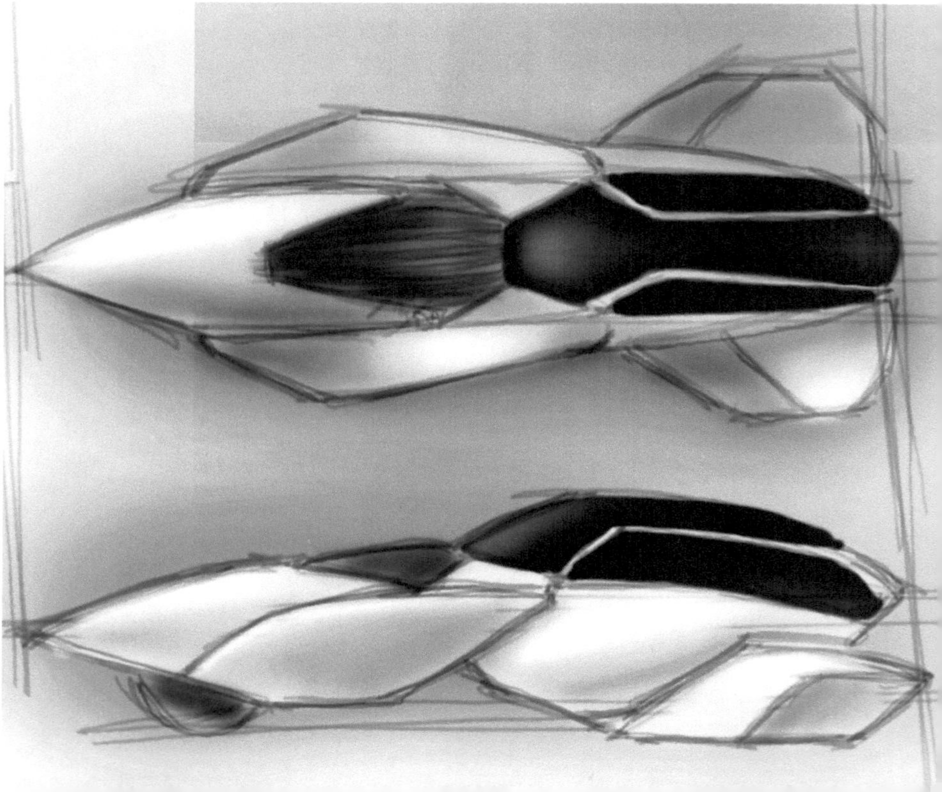

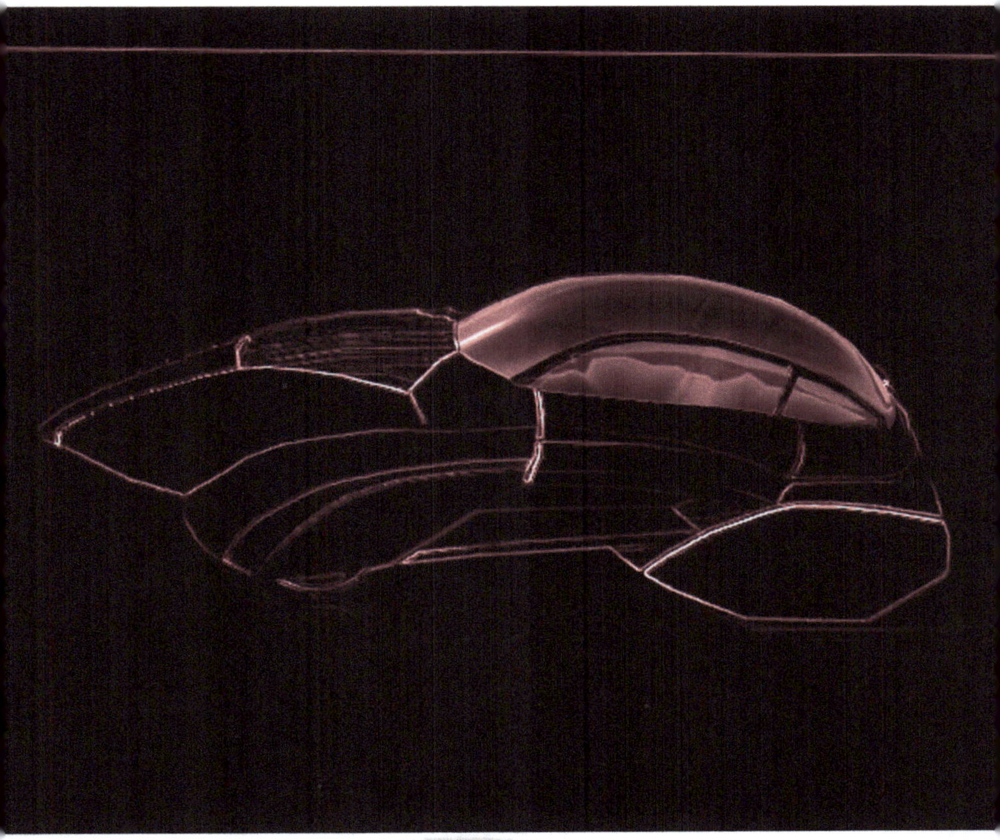

SALLOS

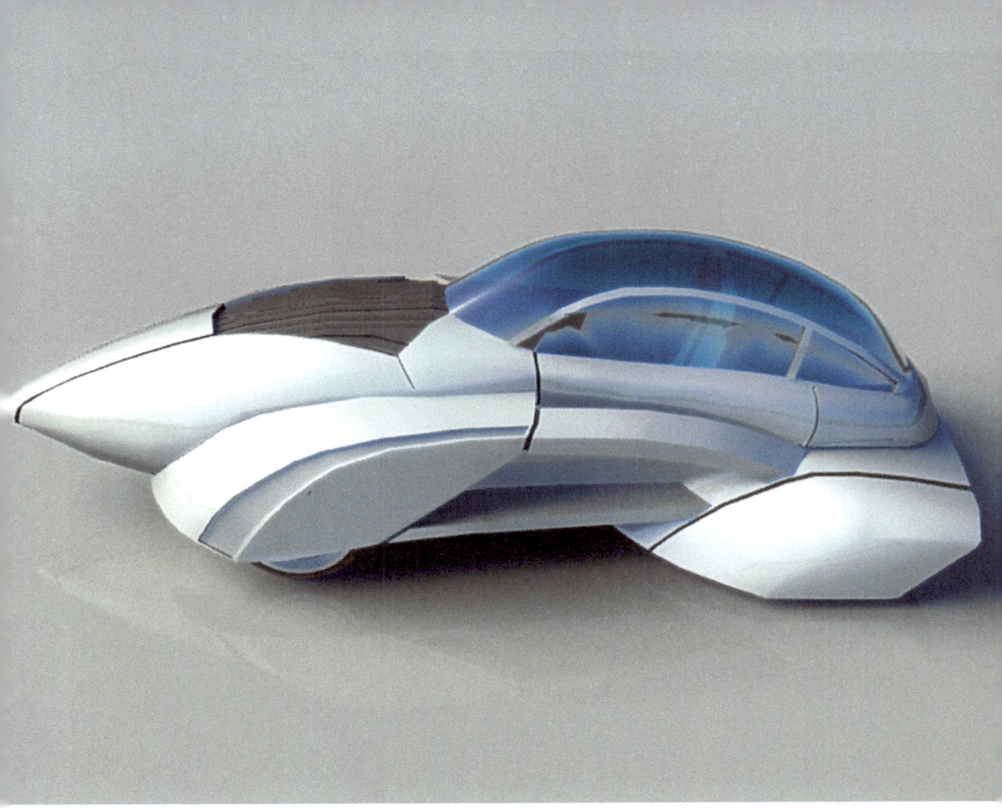

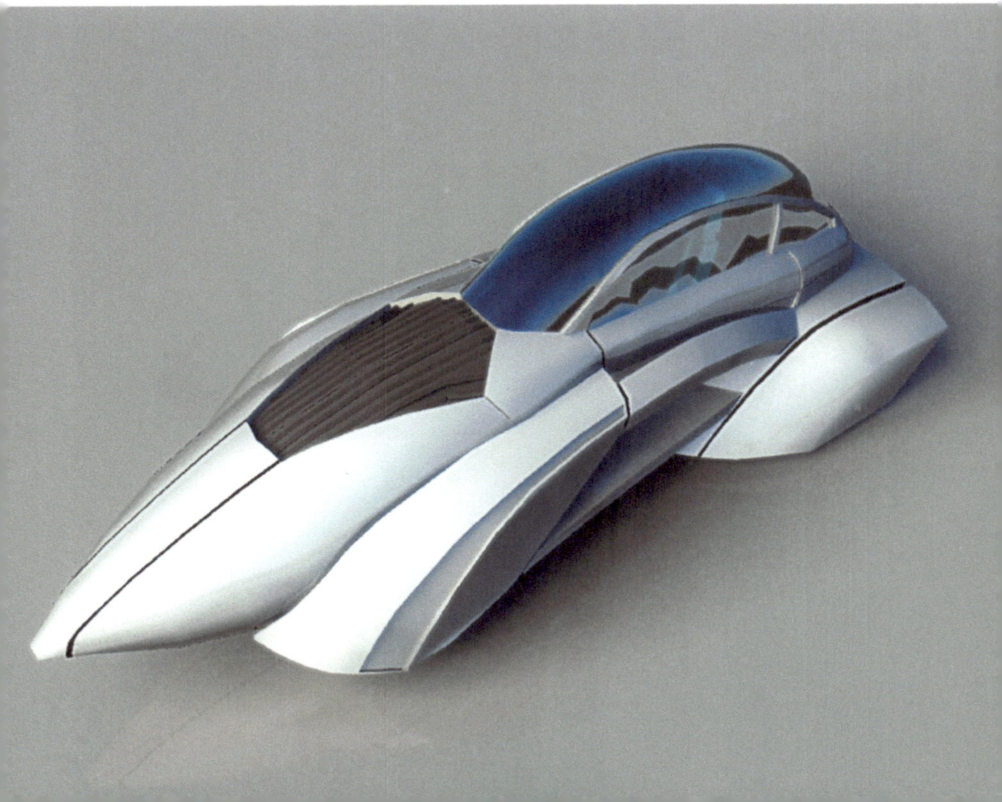

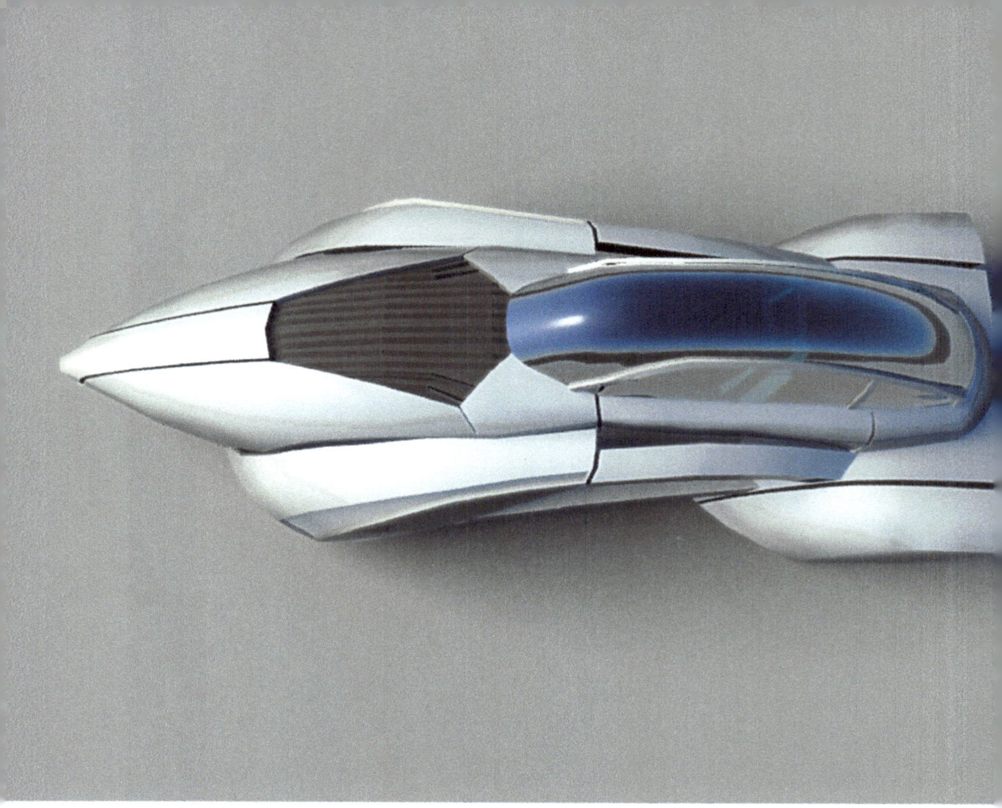

23

24

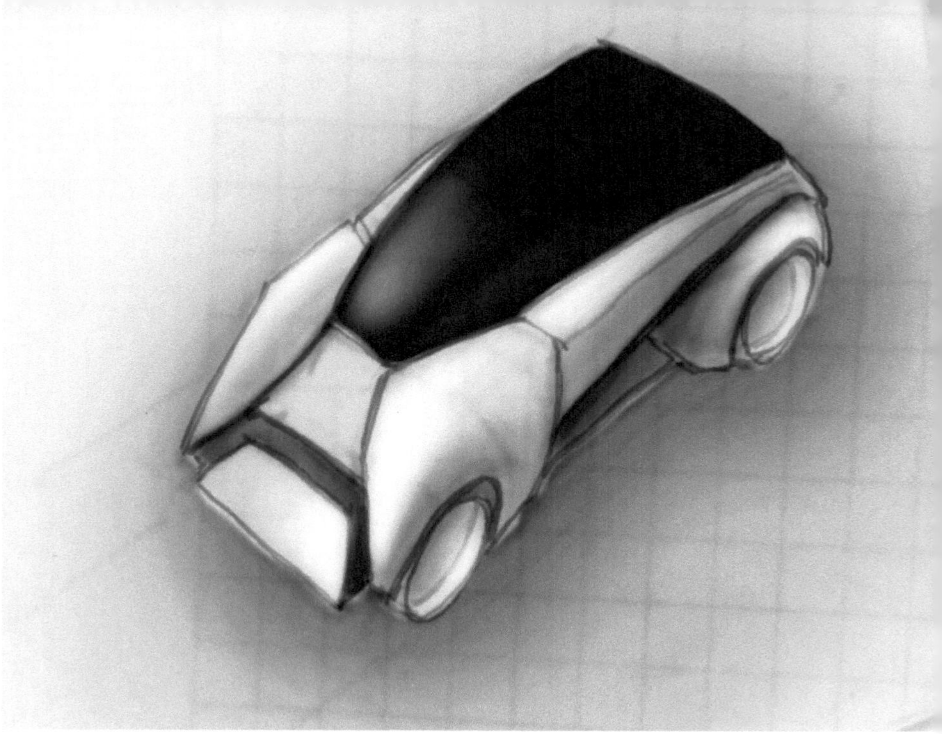

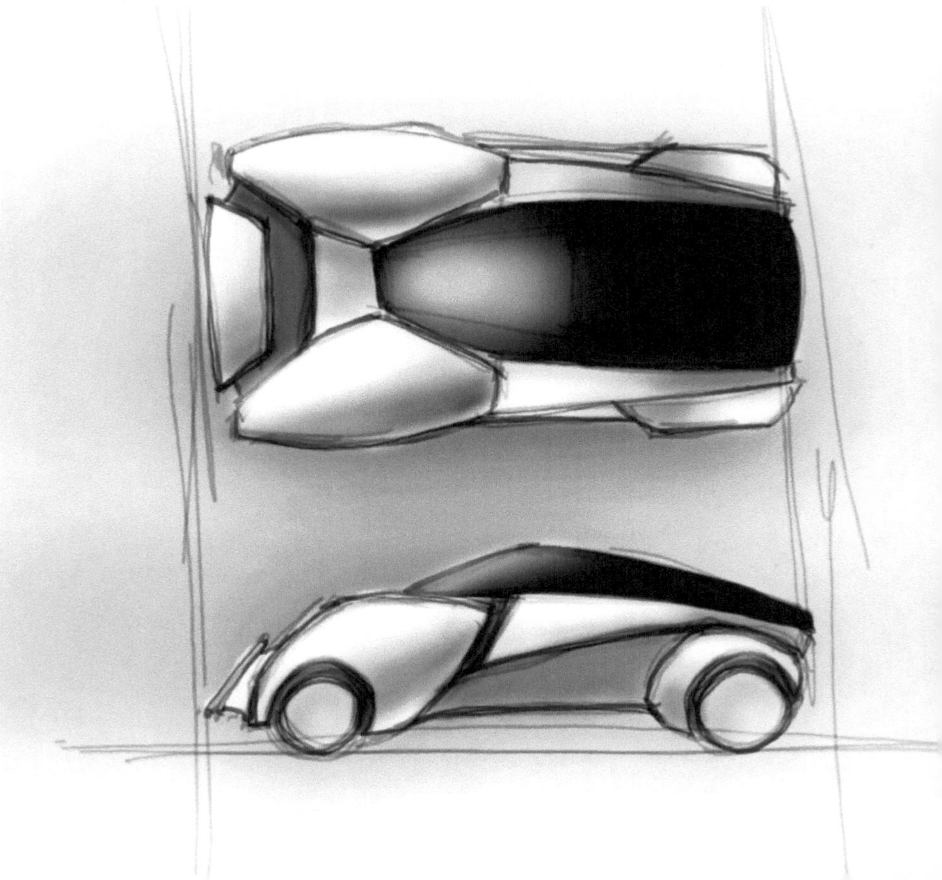

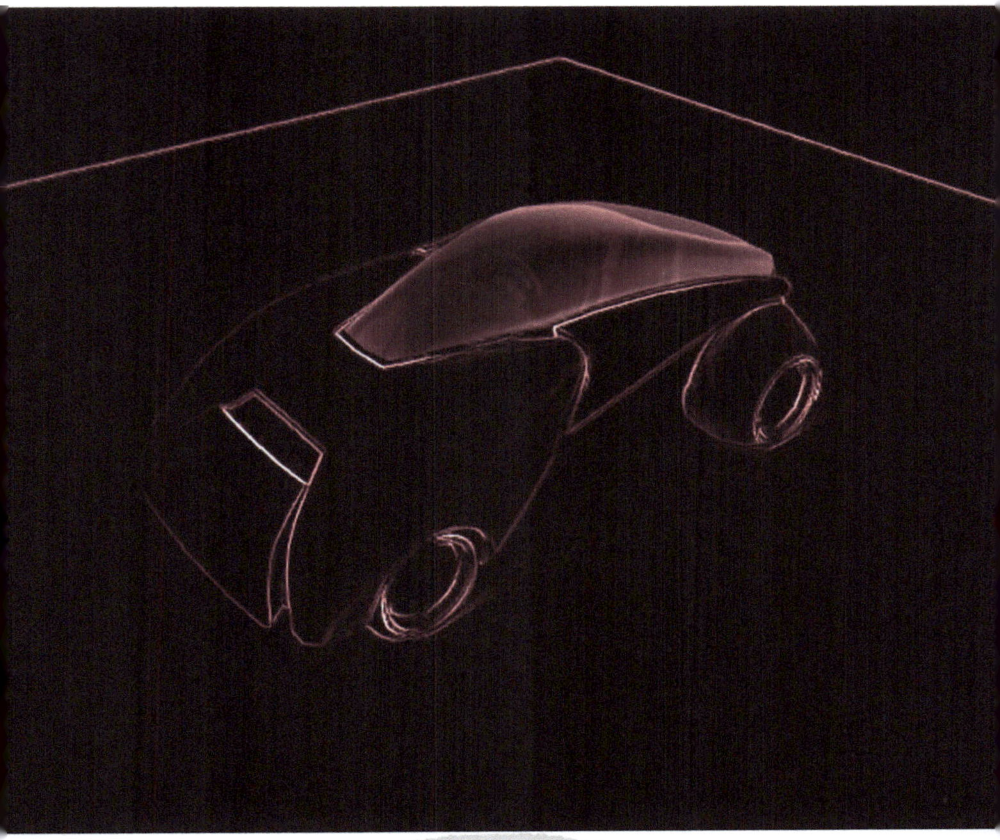

LERAJE

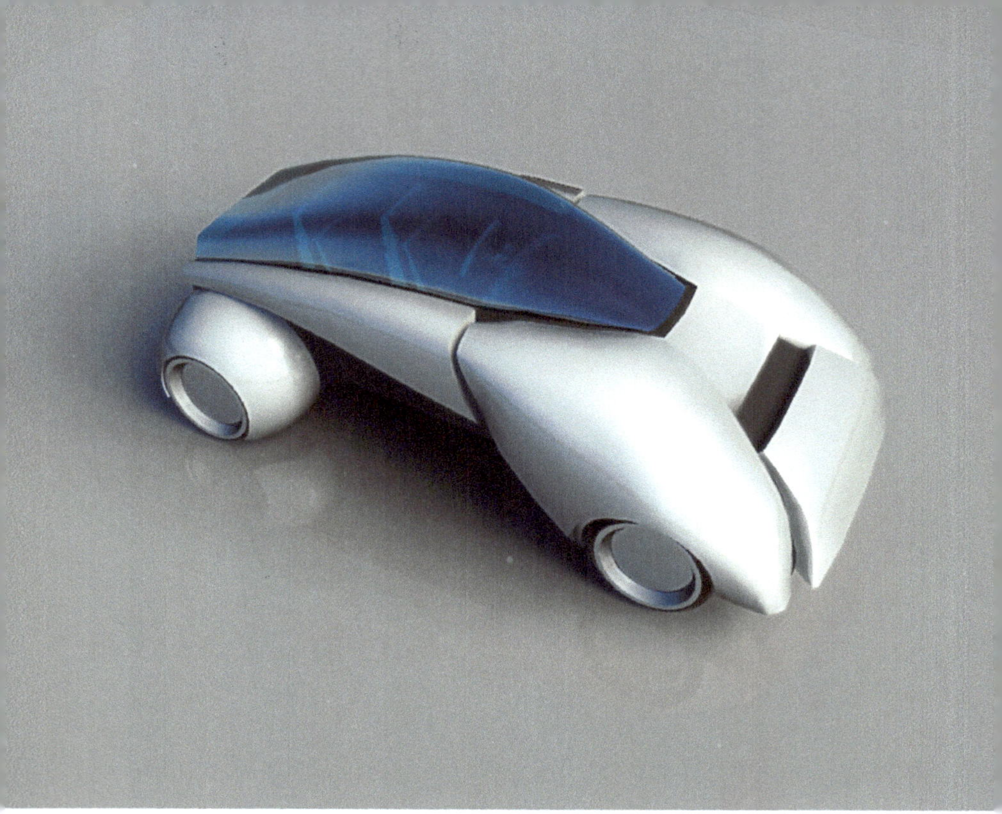

29

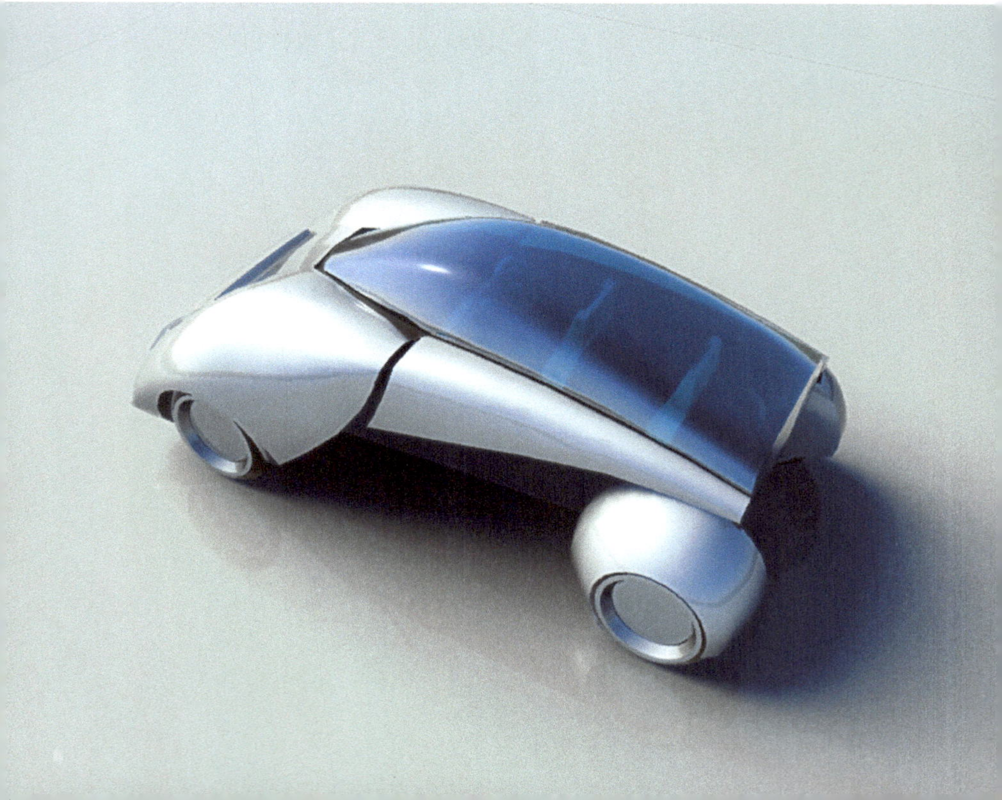

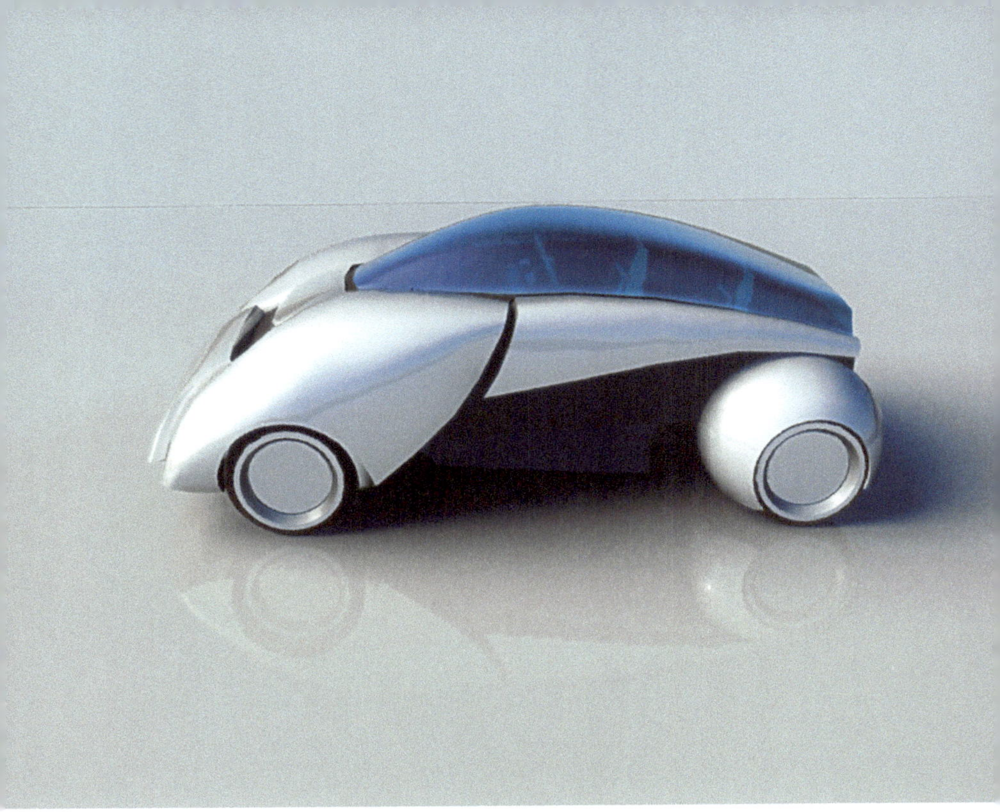

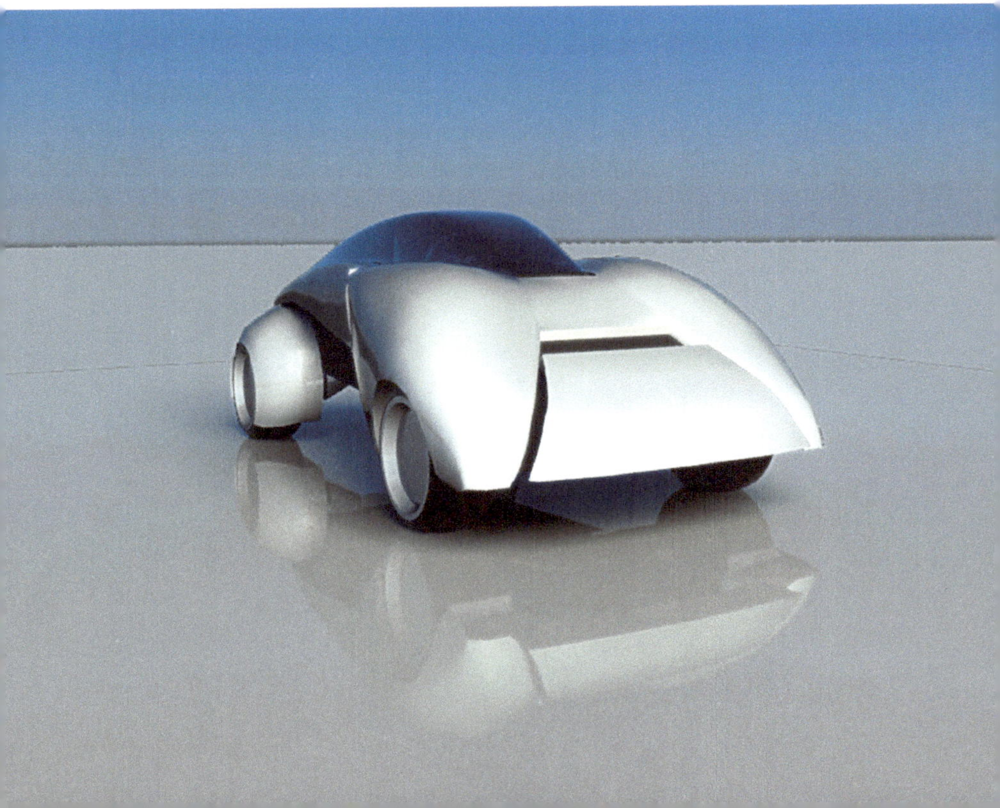

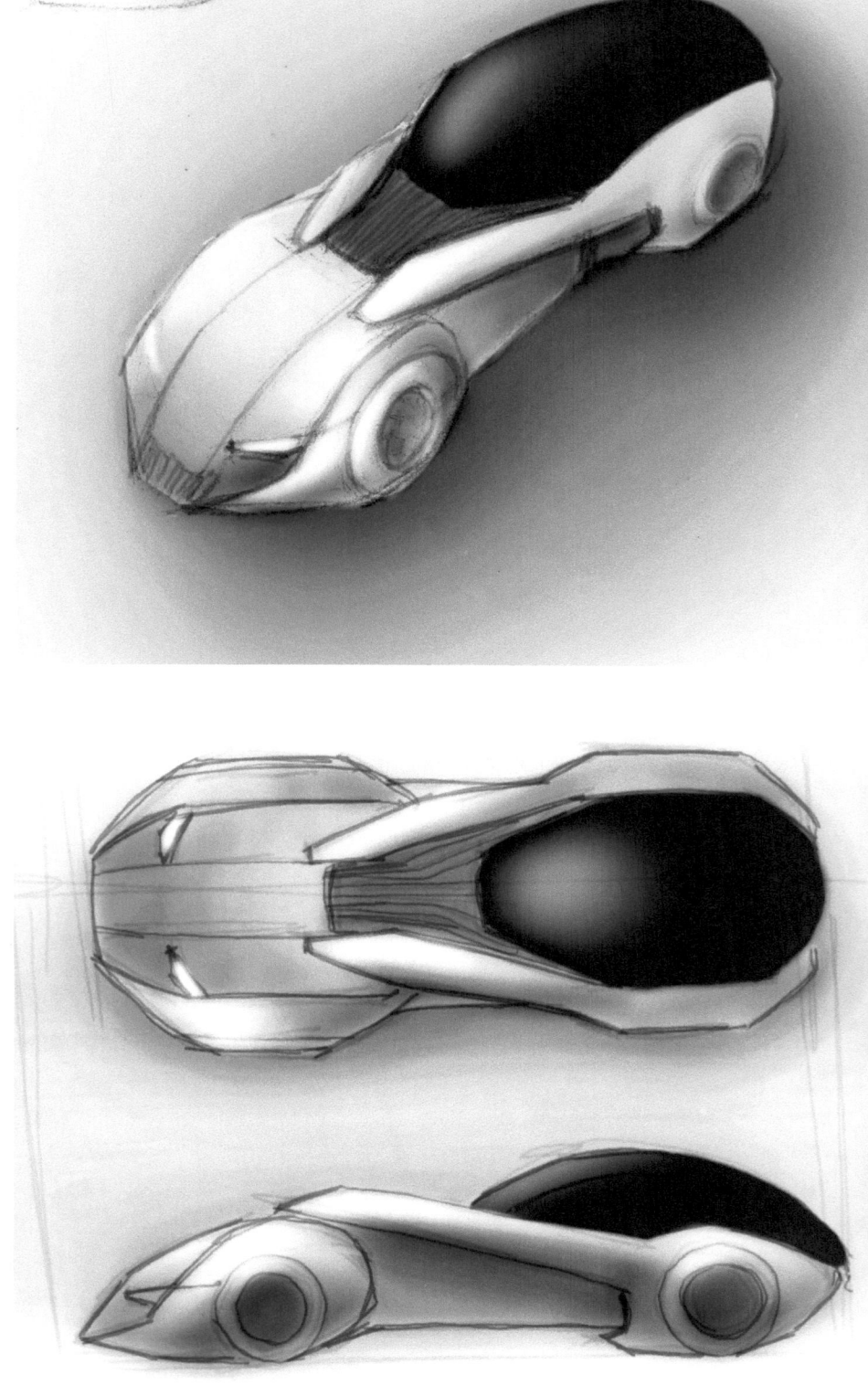

BERITH

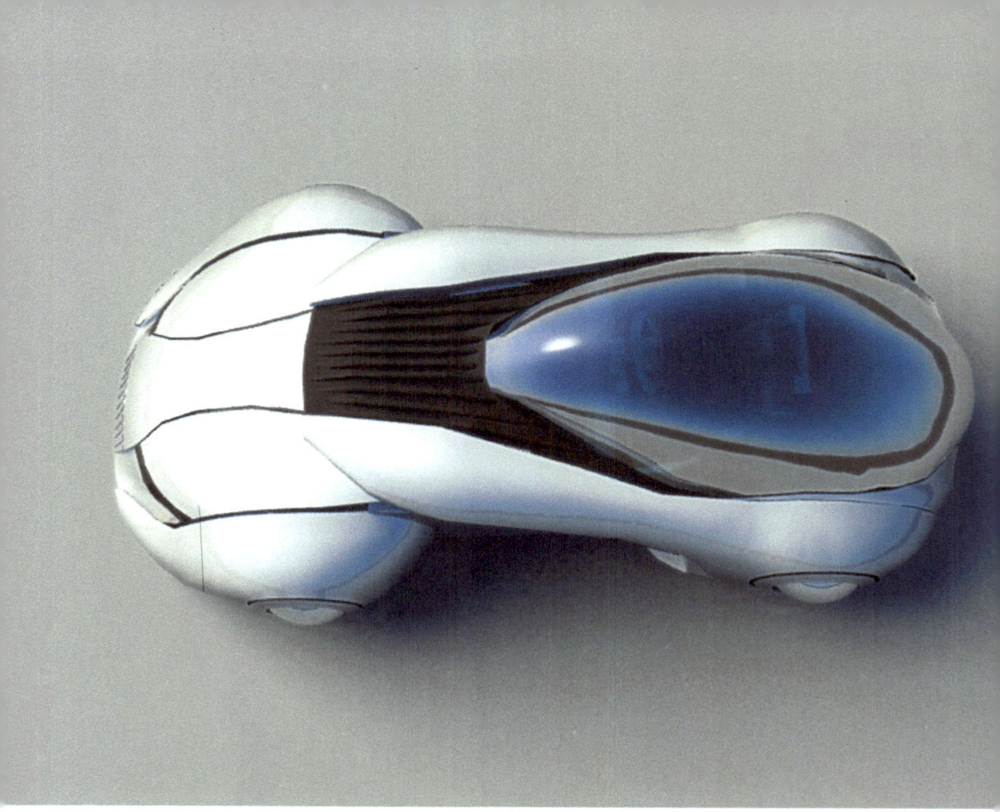

33

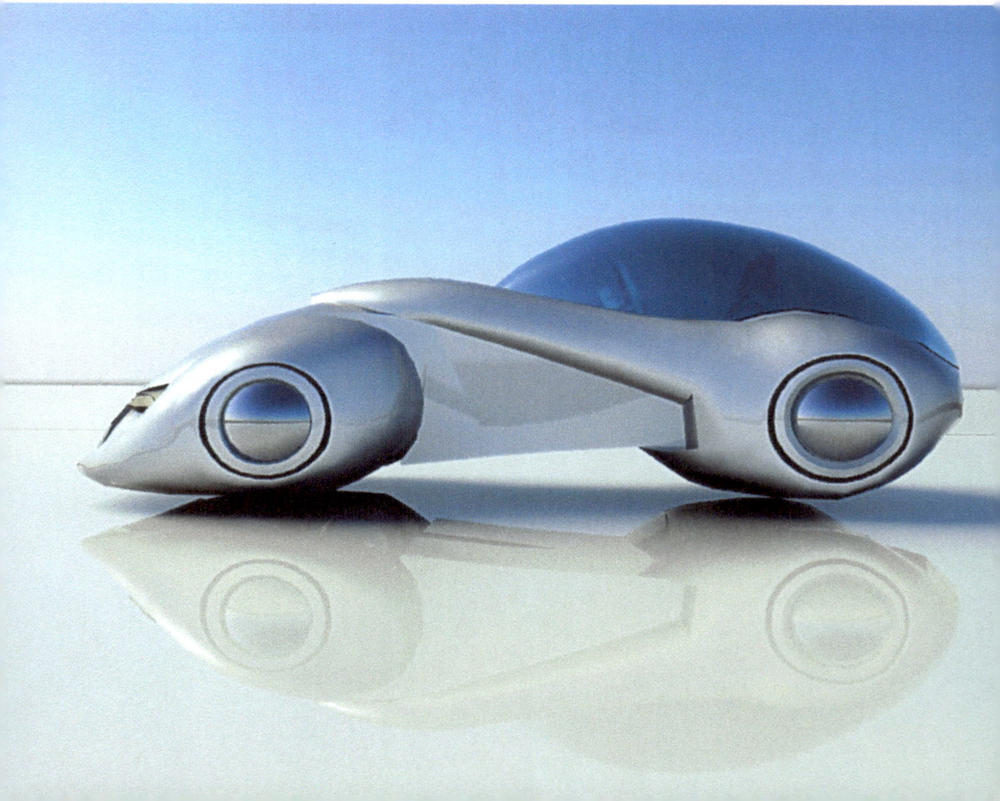

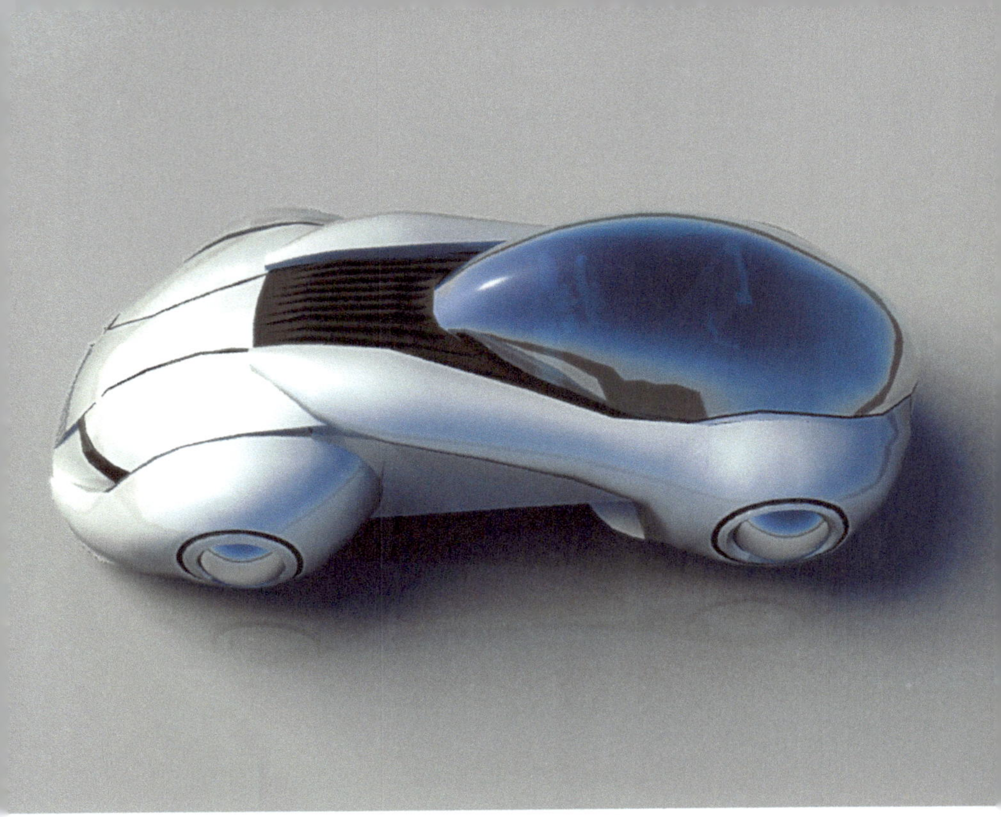

34

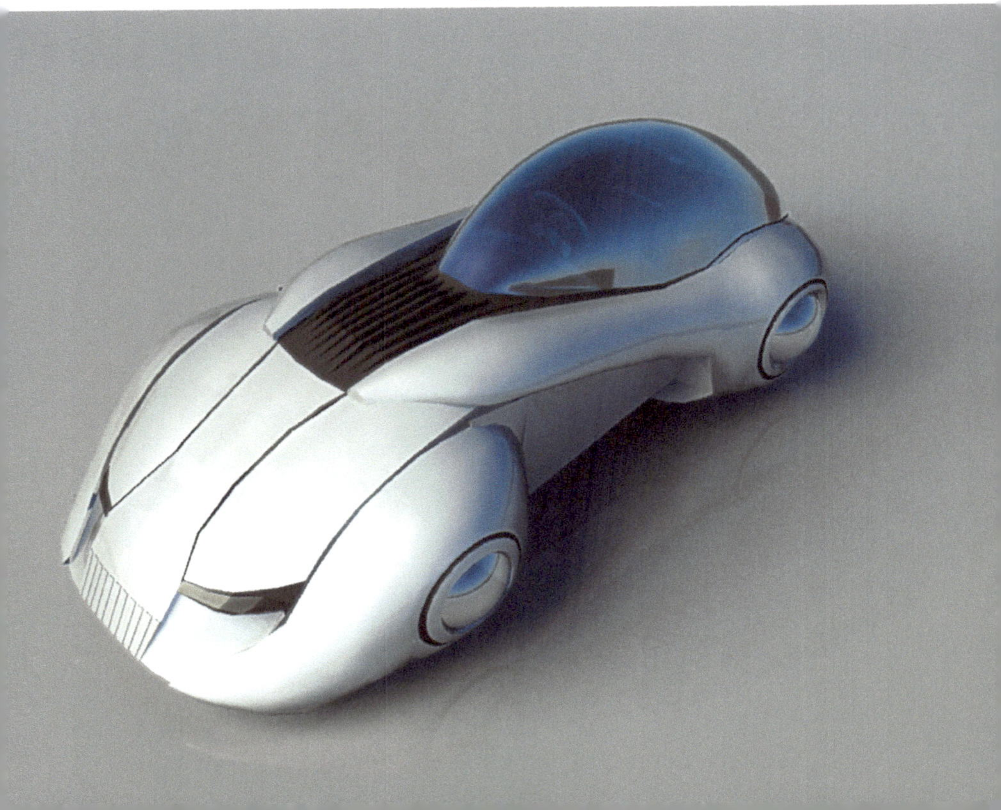

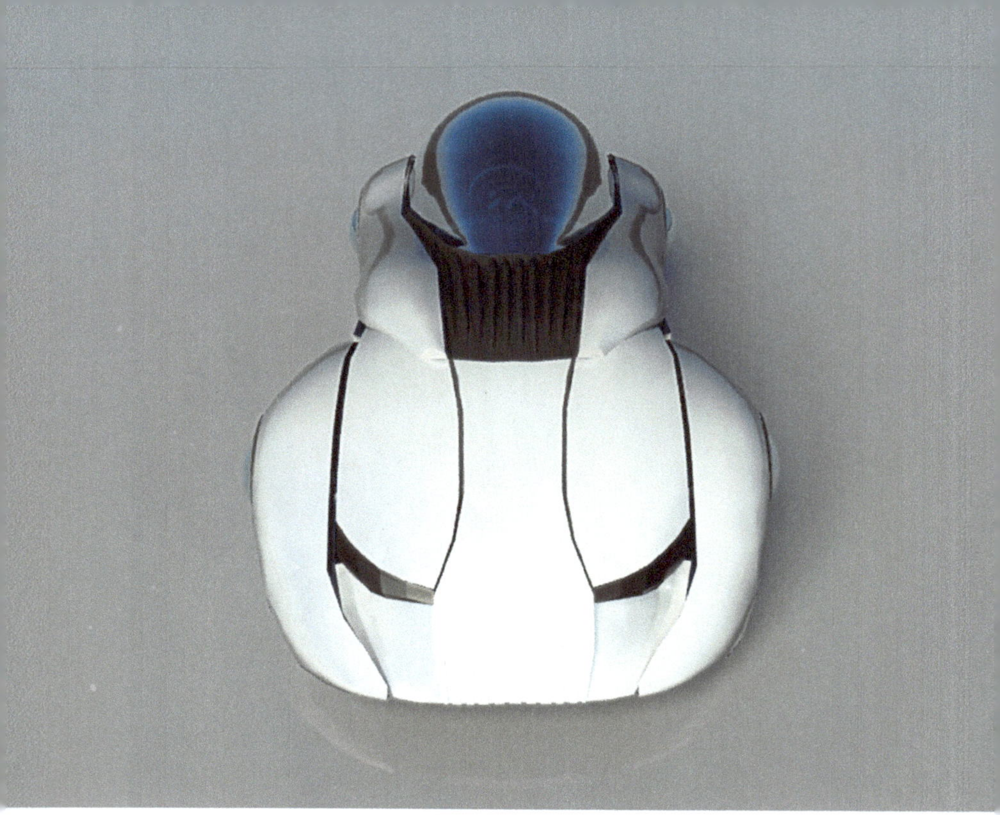

35

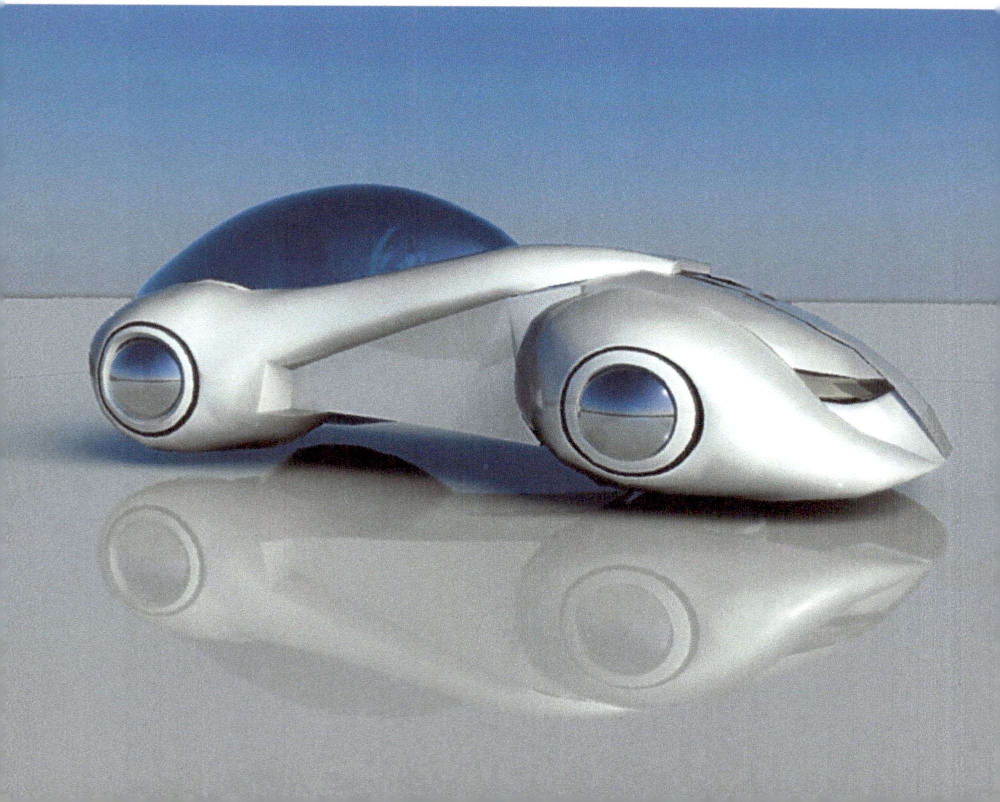

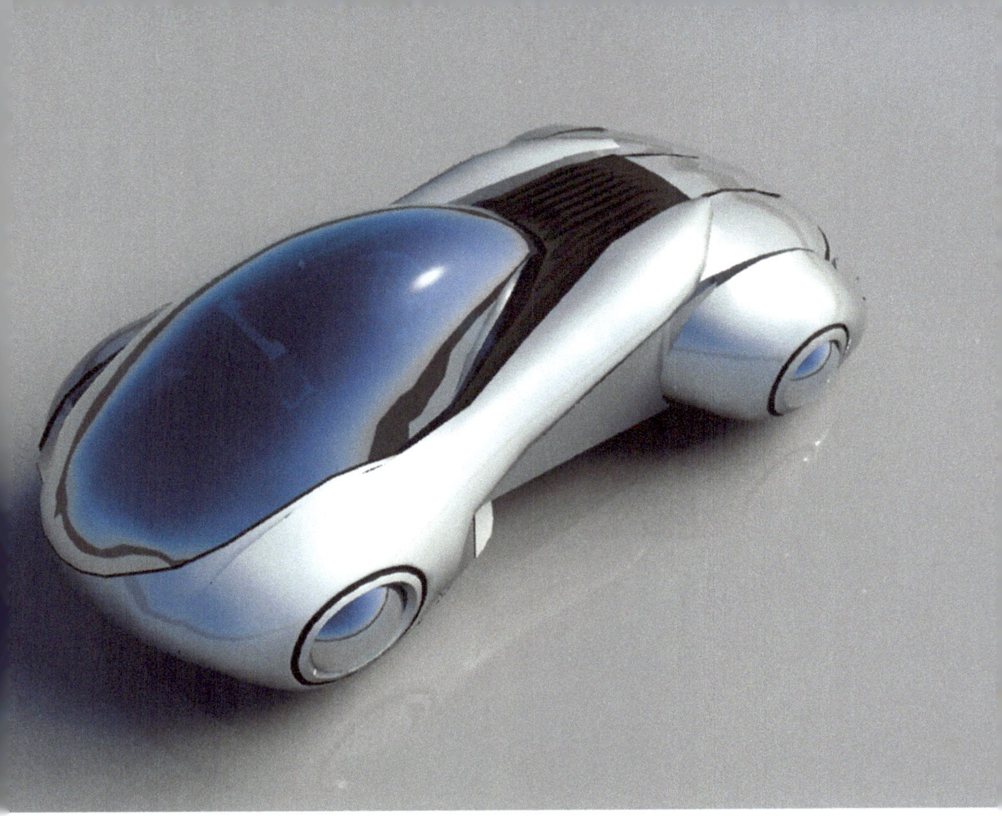

36

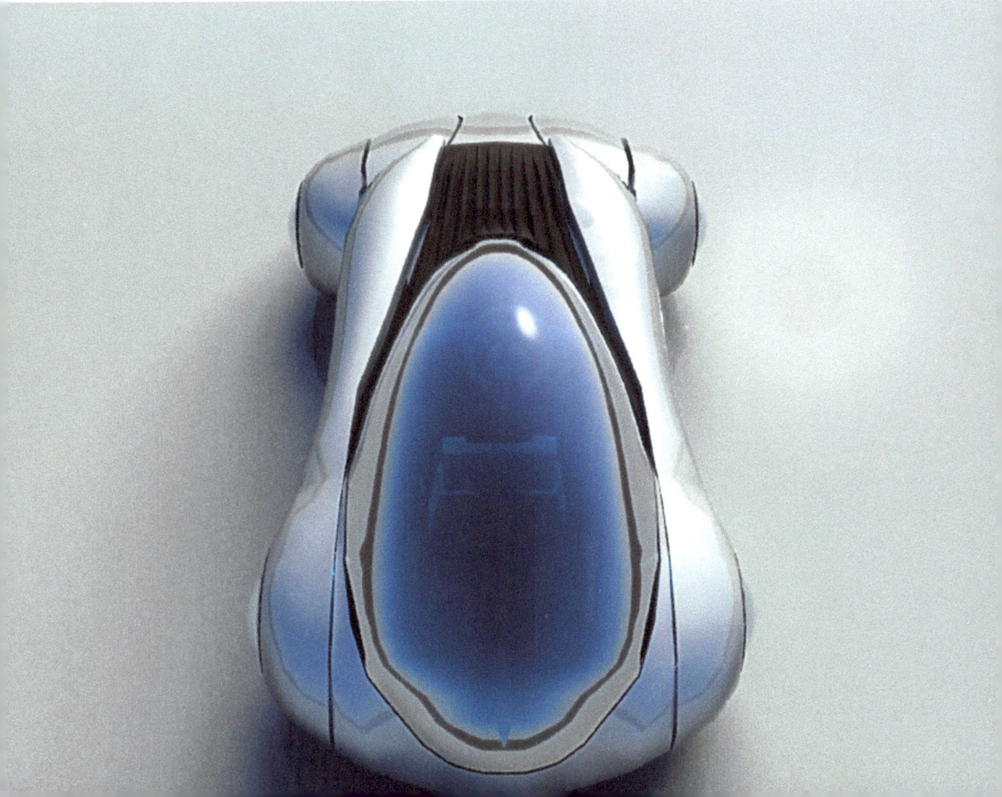

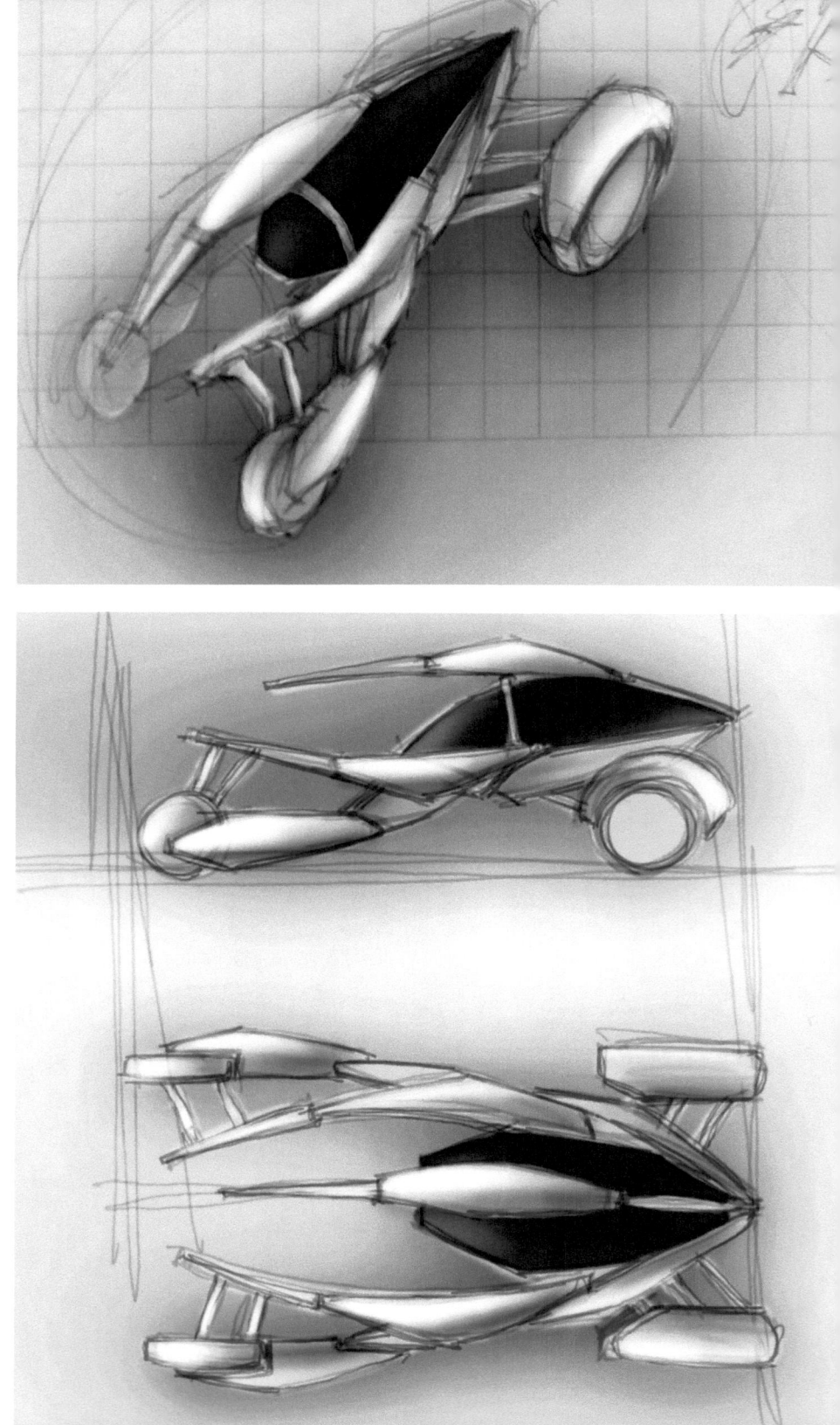

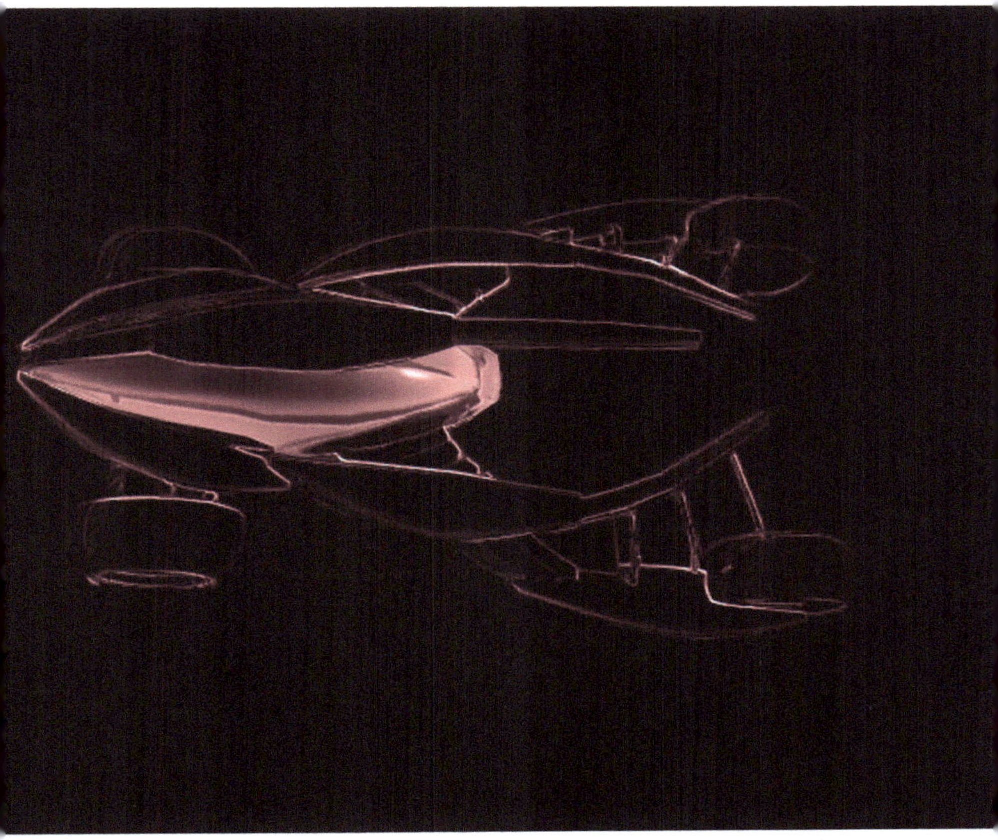

VALEFOR

39

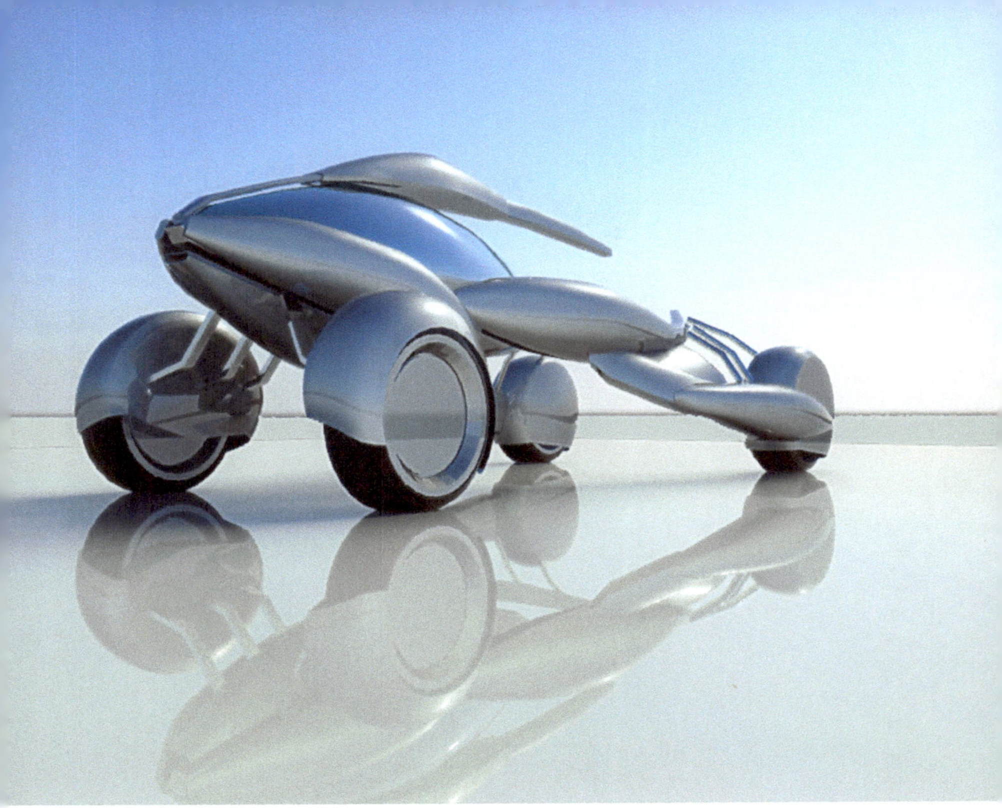

40

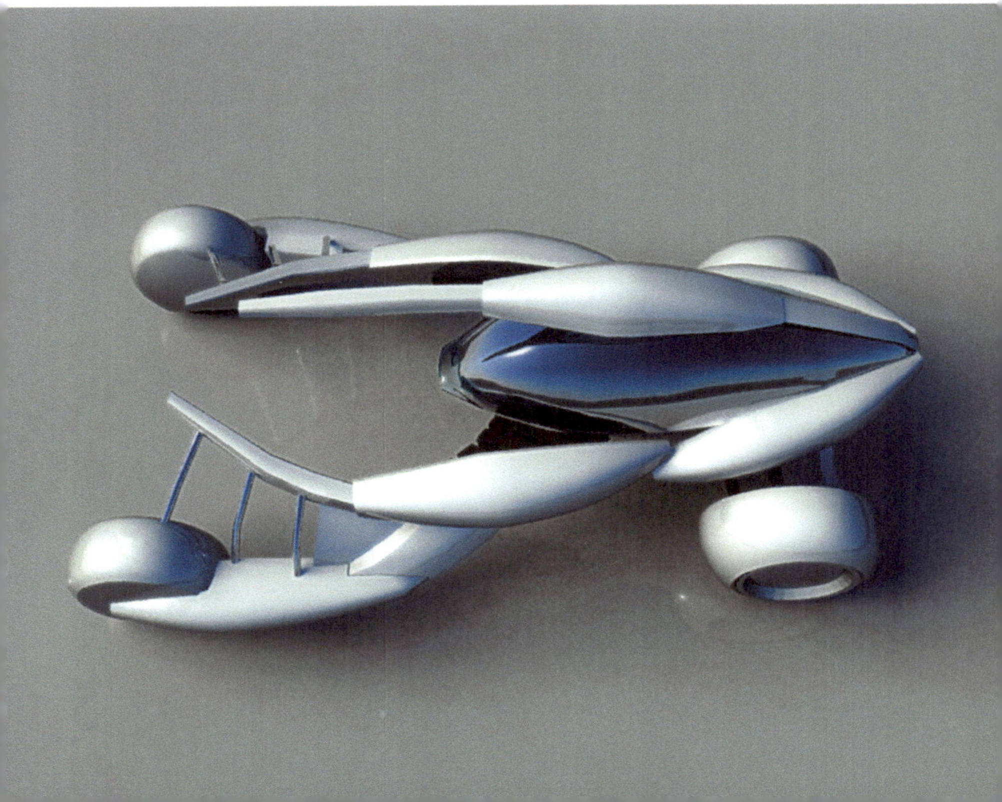

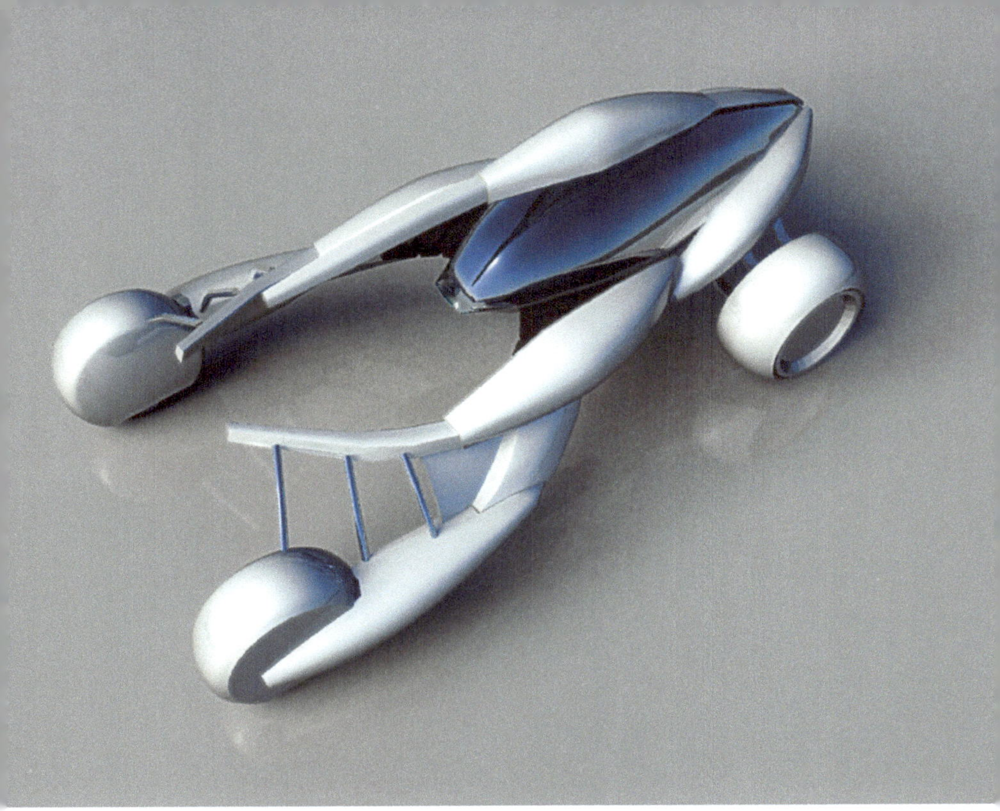

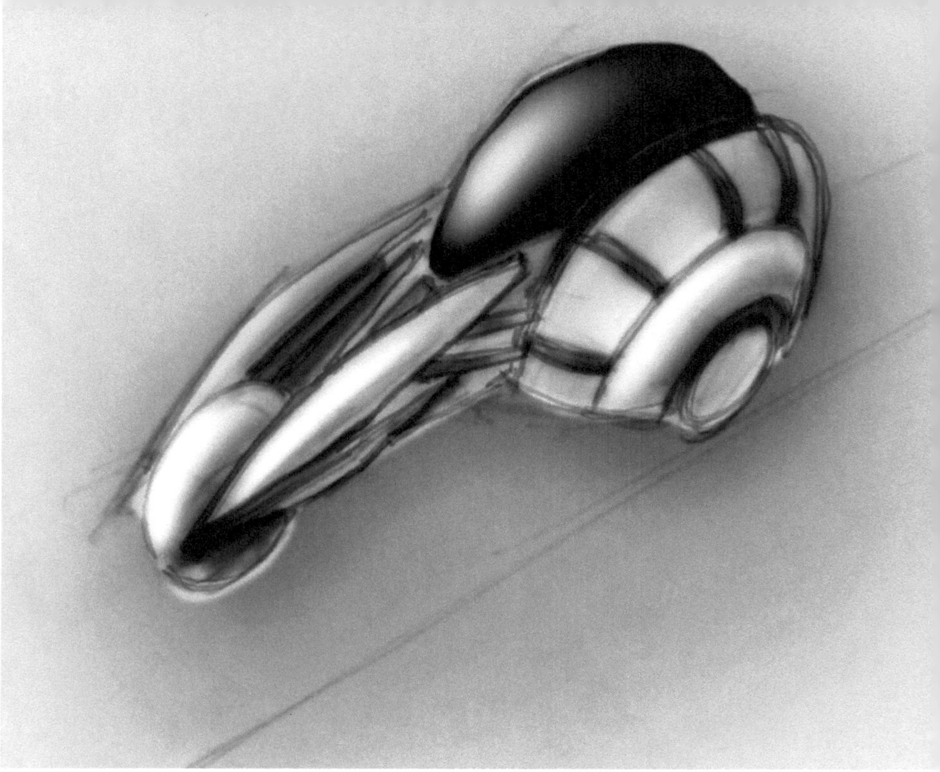

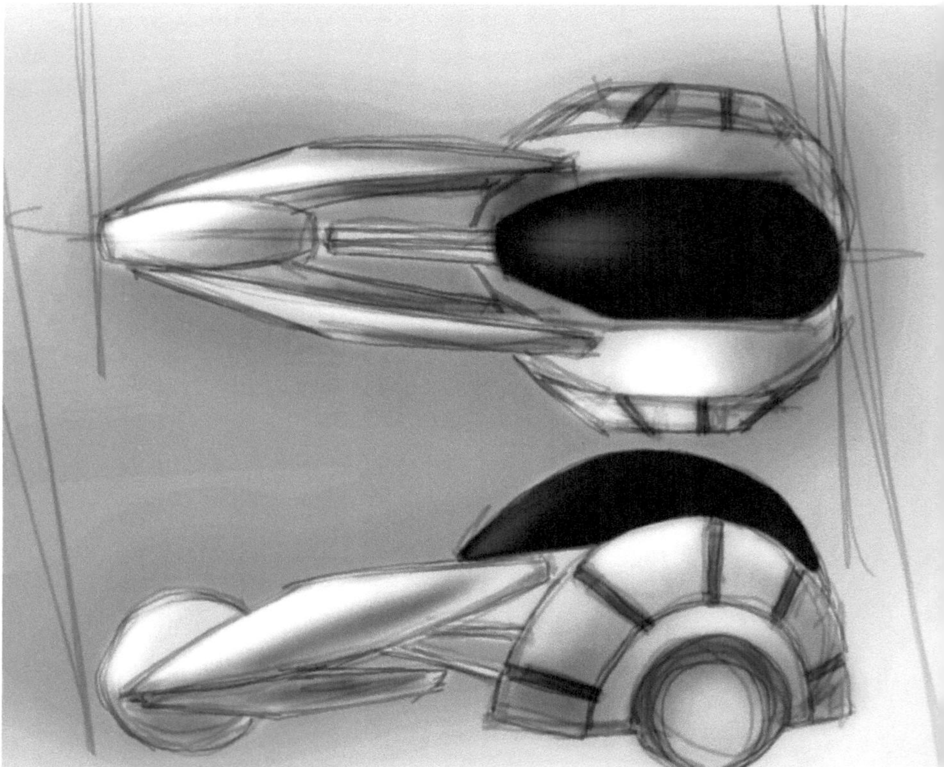

ELIGOS

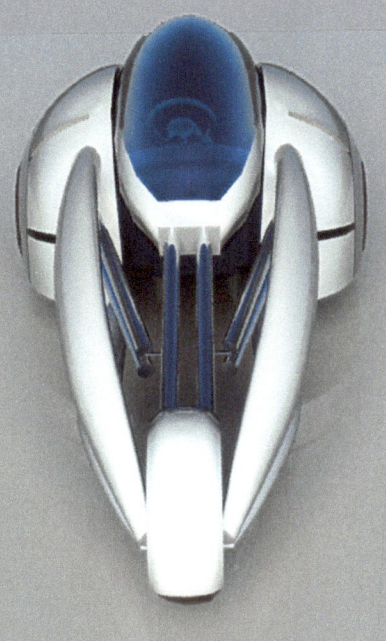

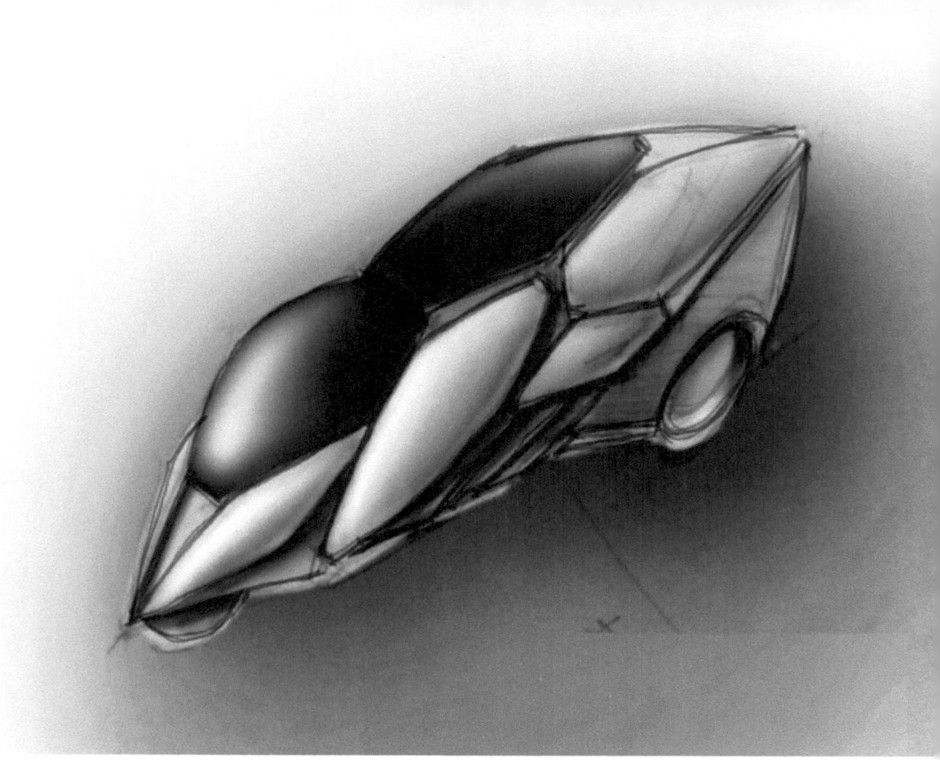

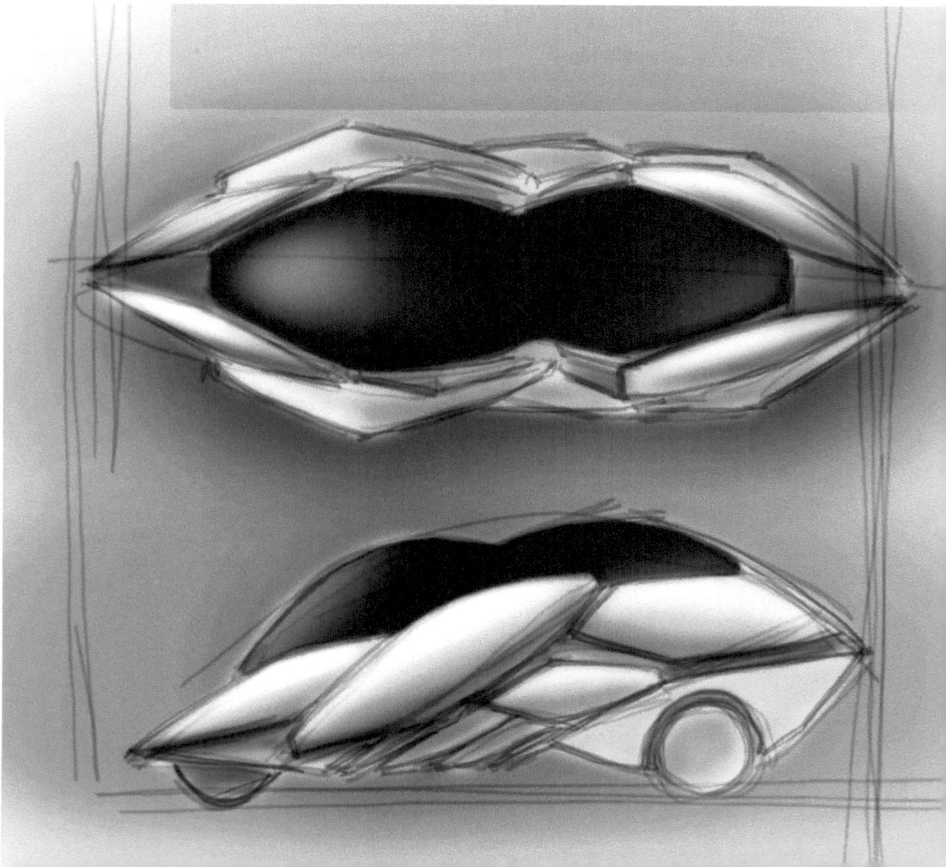

NABERIUS

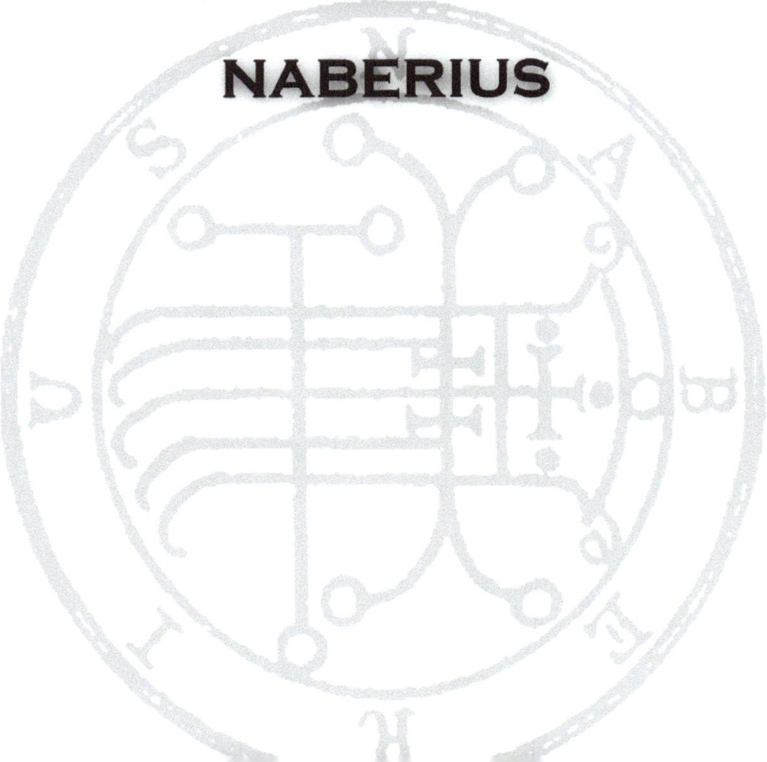

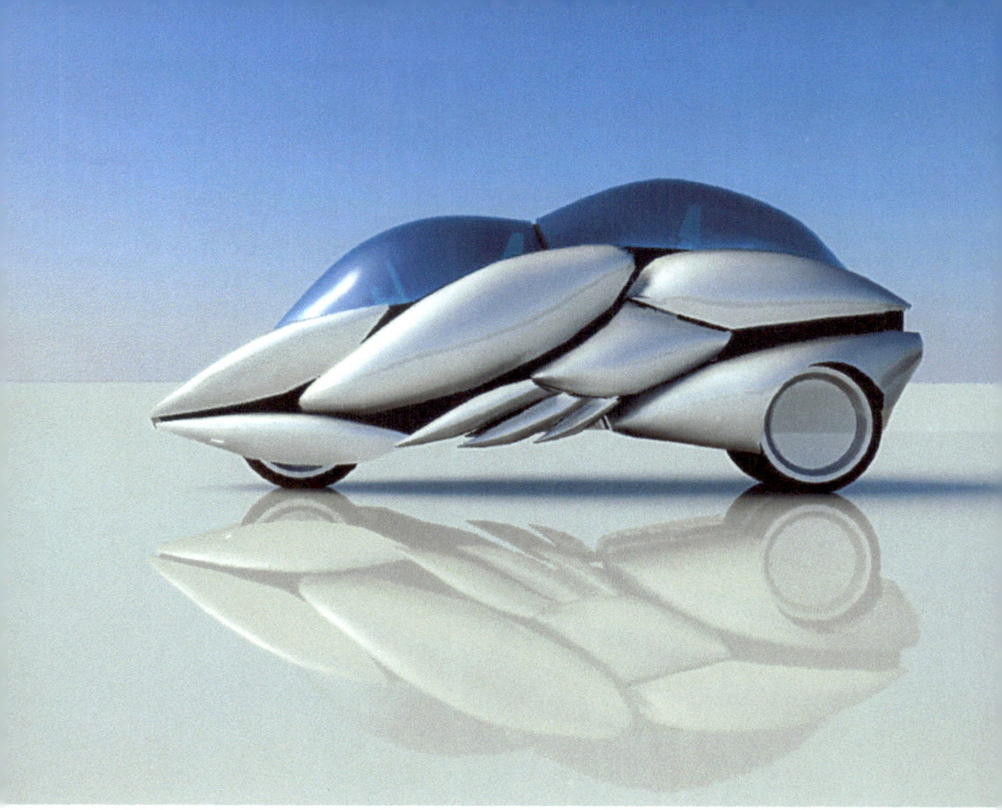

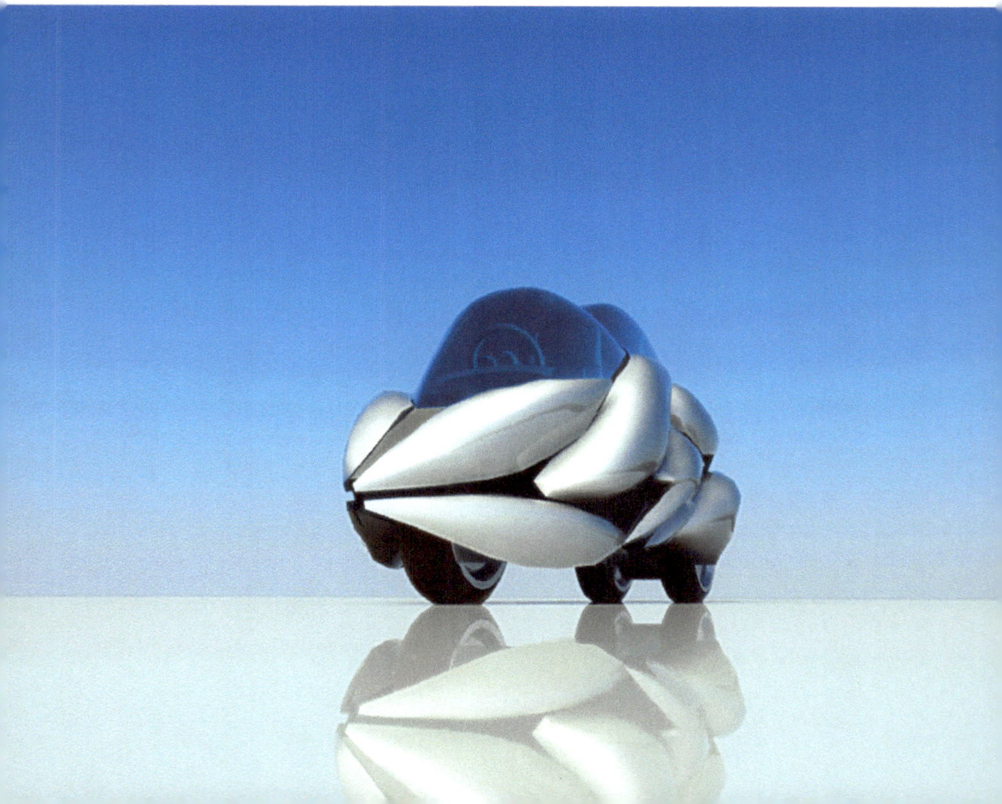

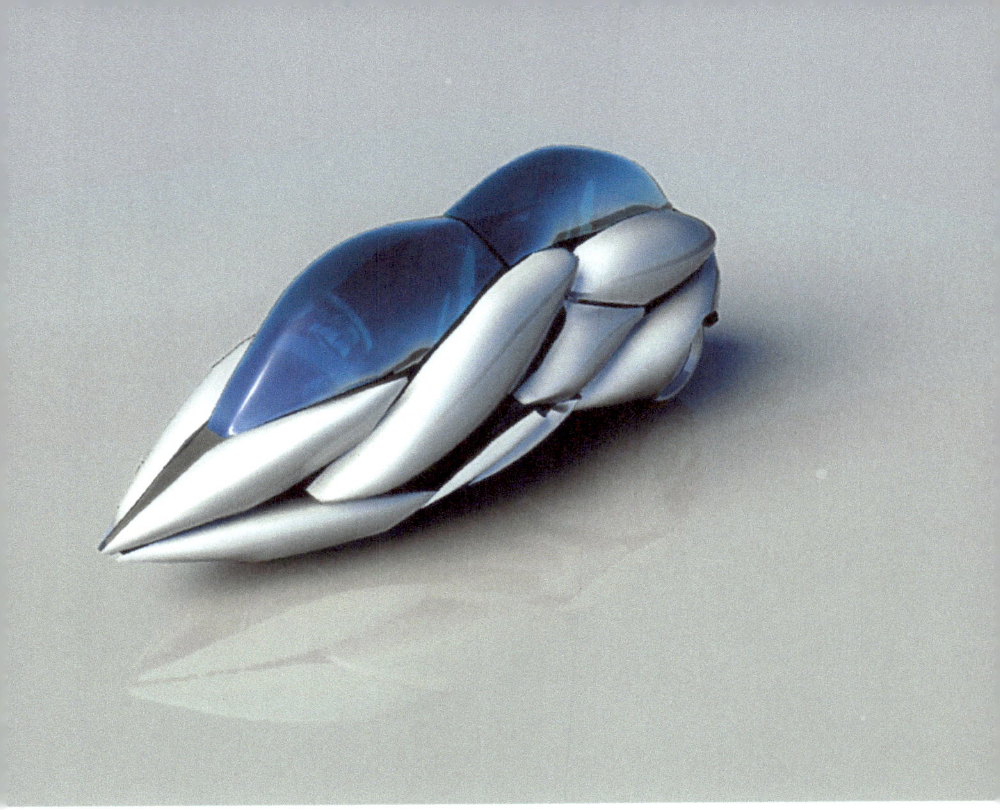

52

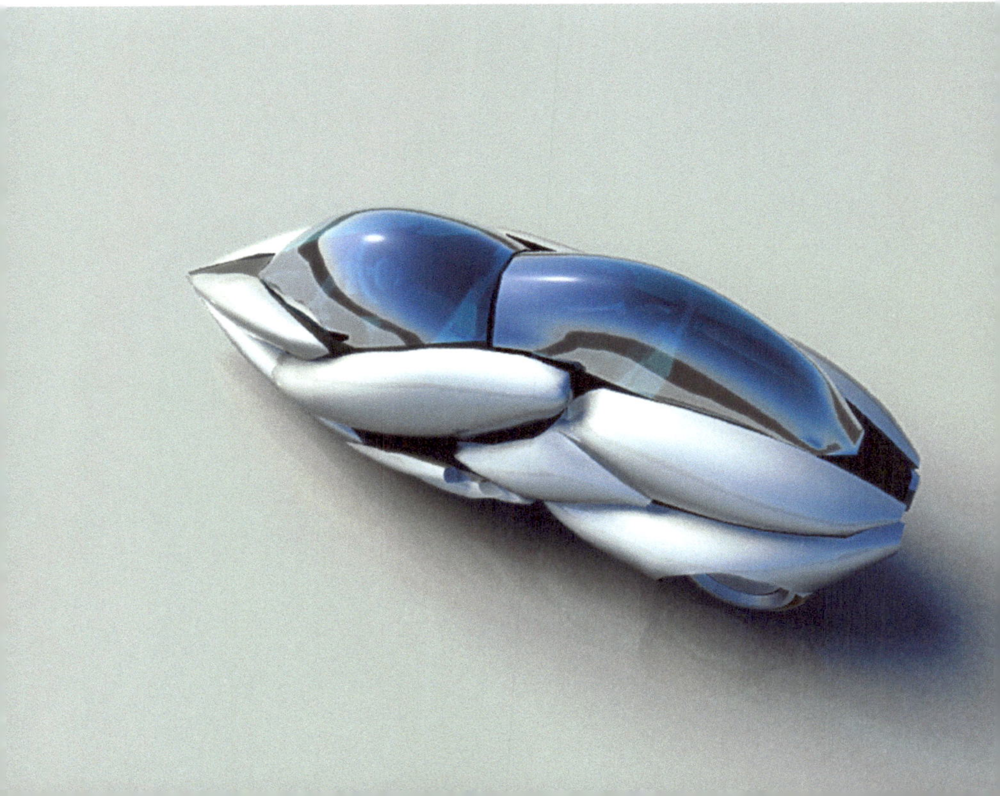

53

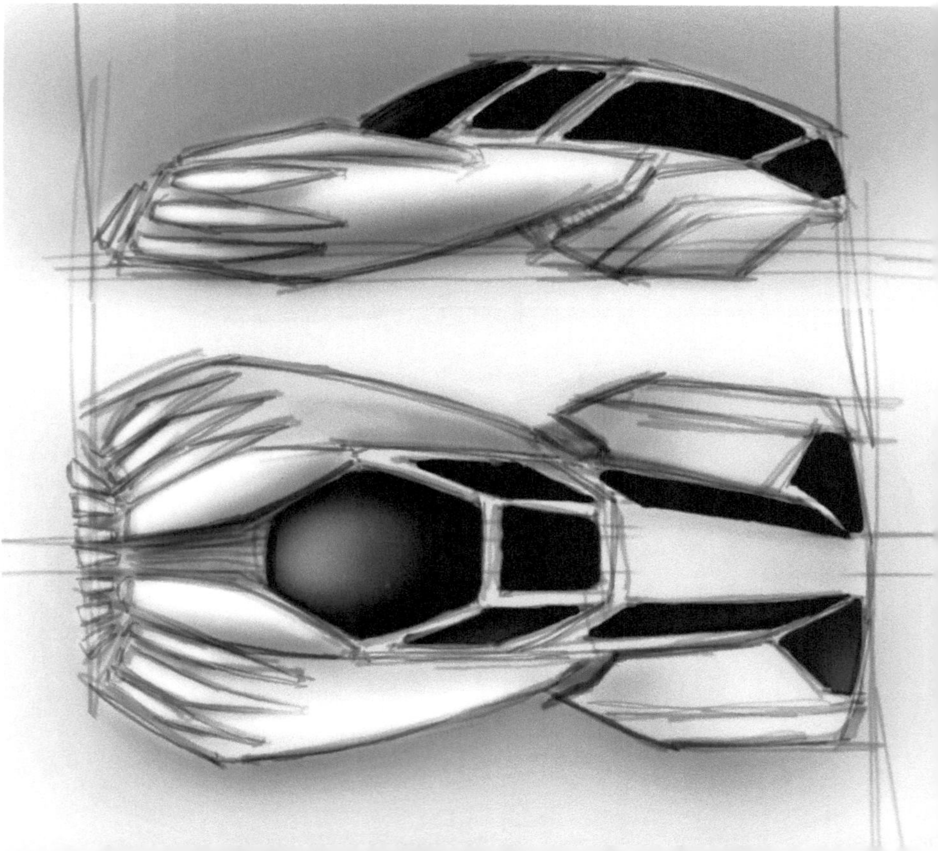

BIFRONS

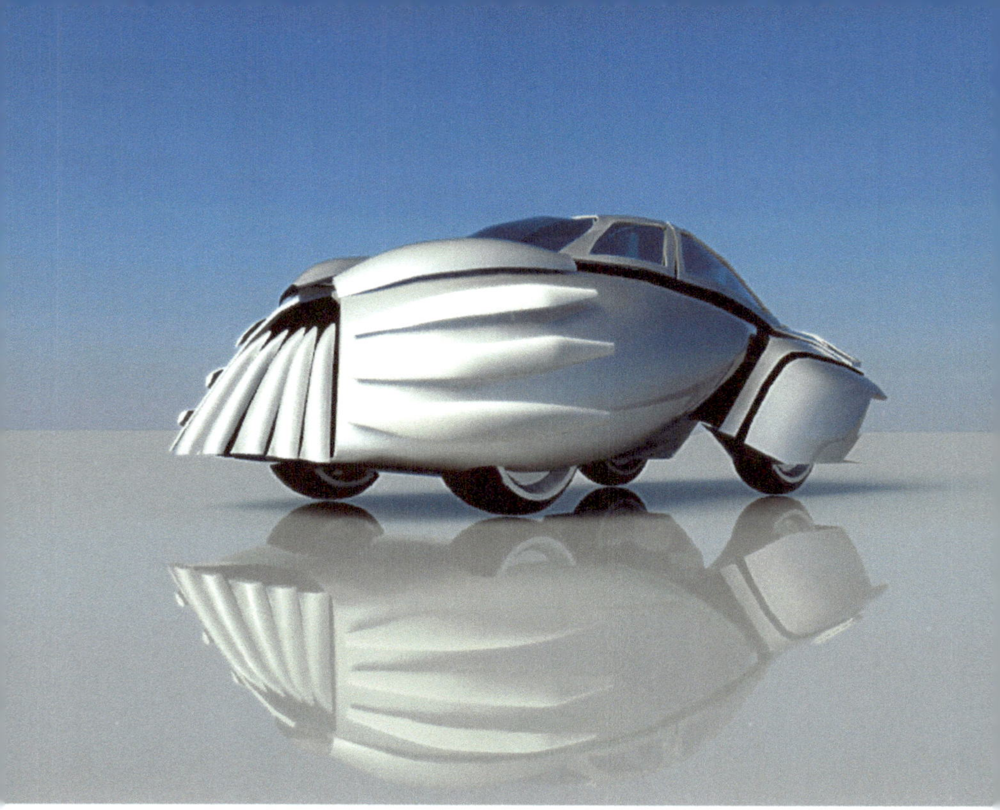

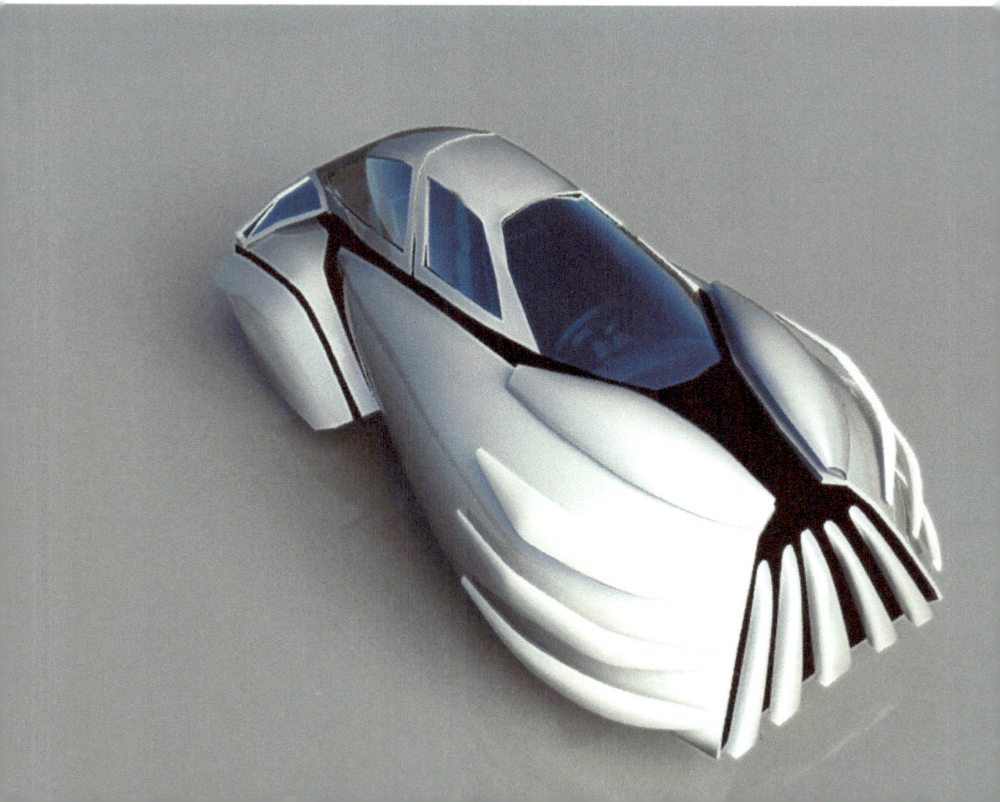

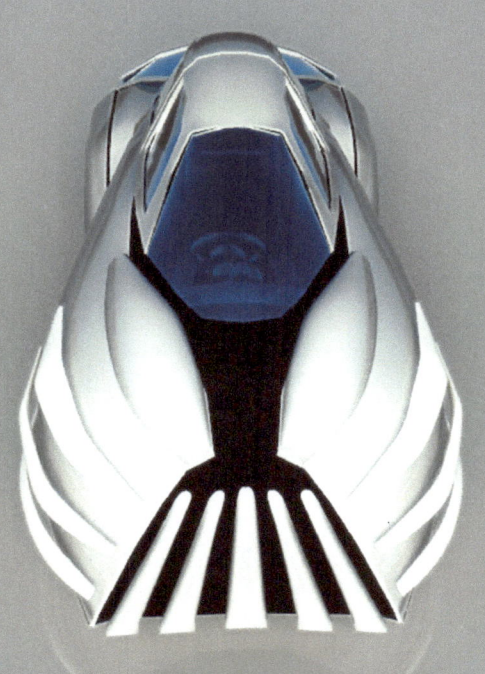

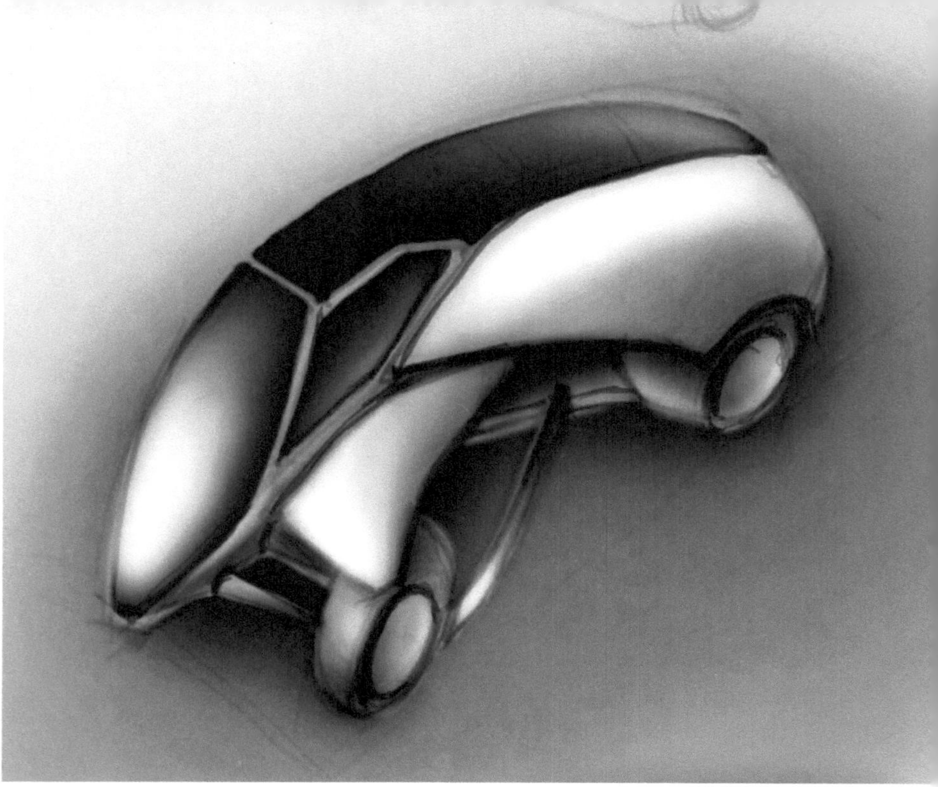

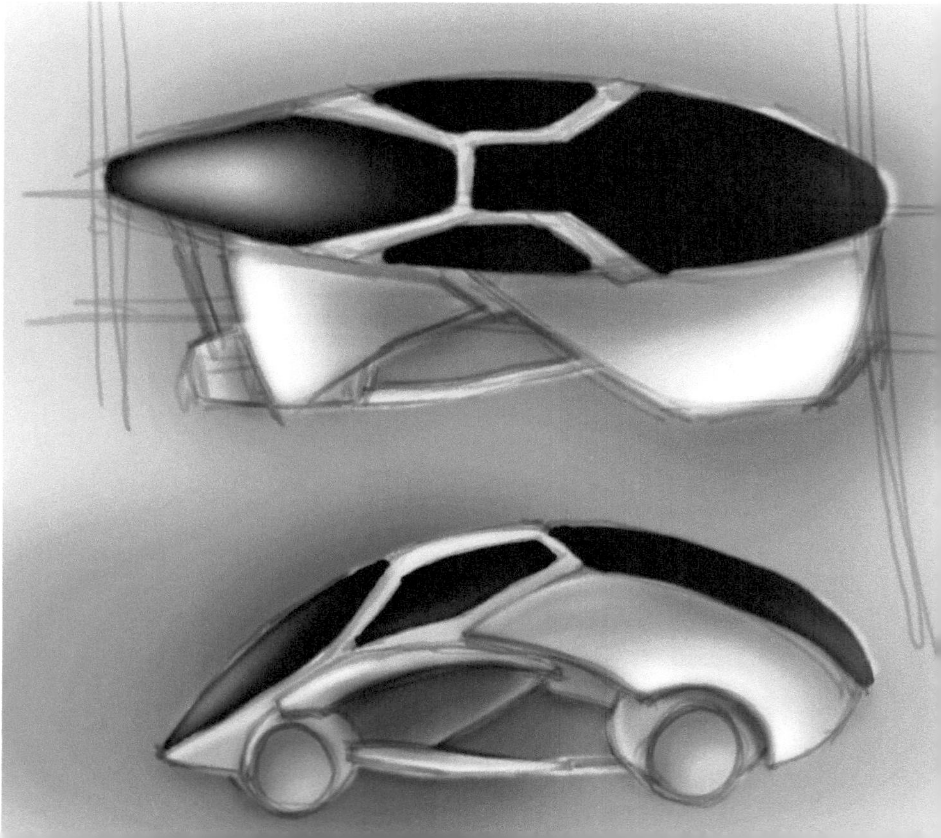

CROCELL

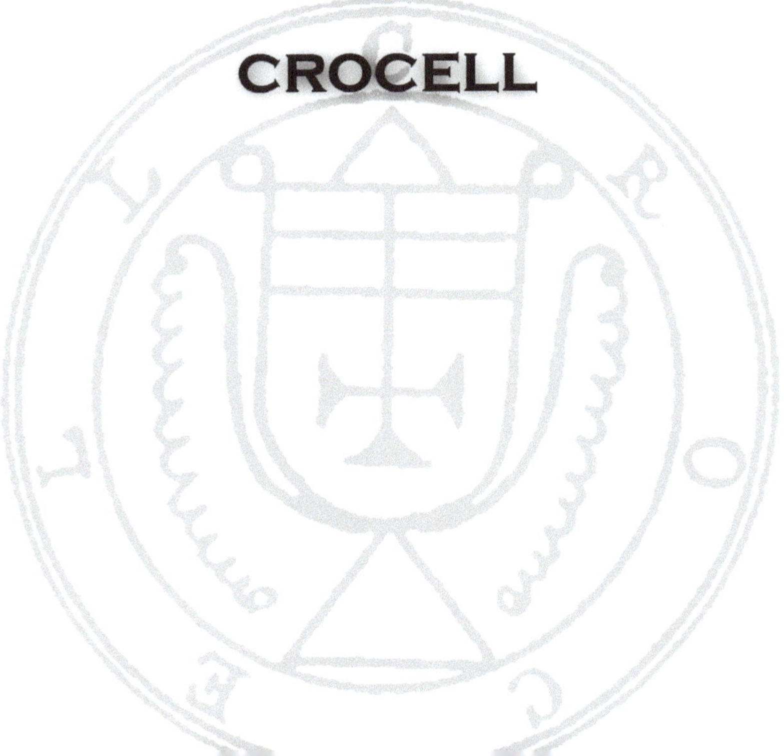

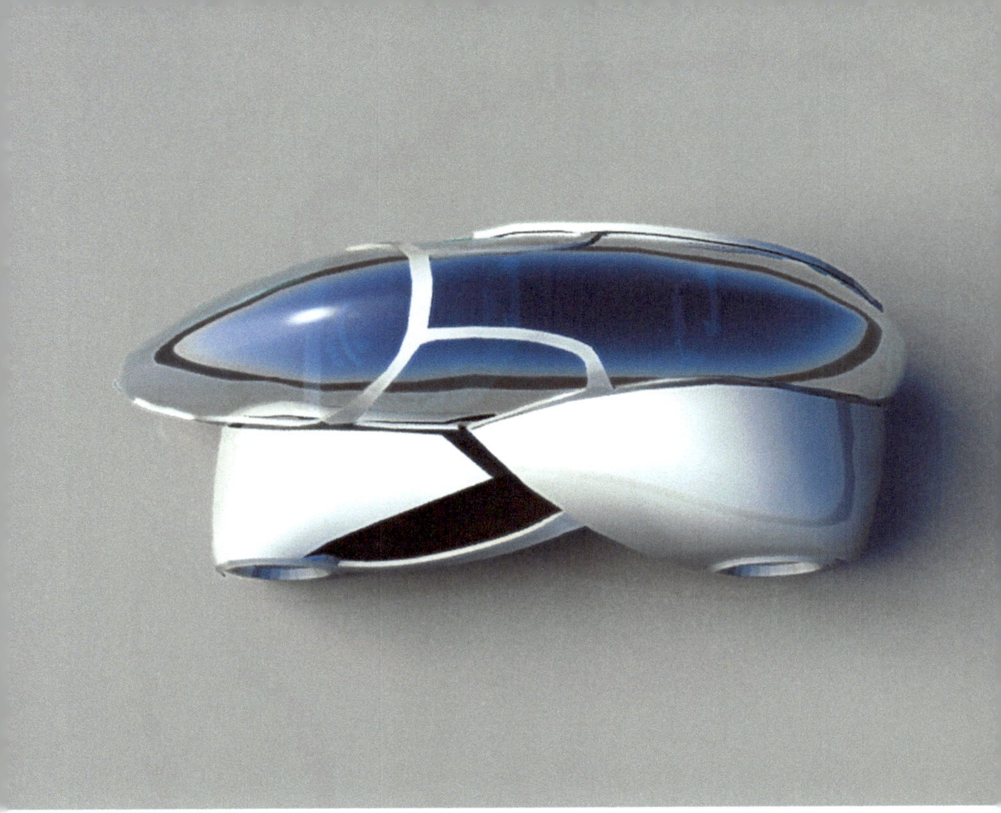

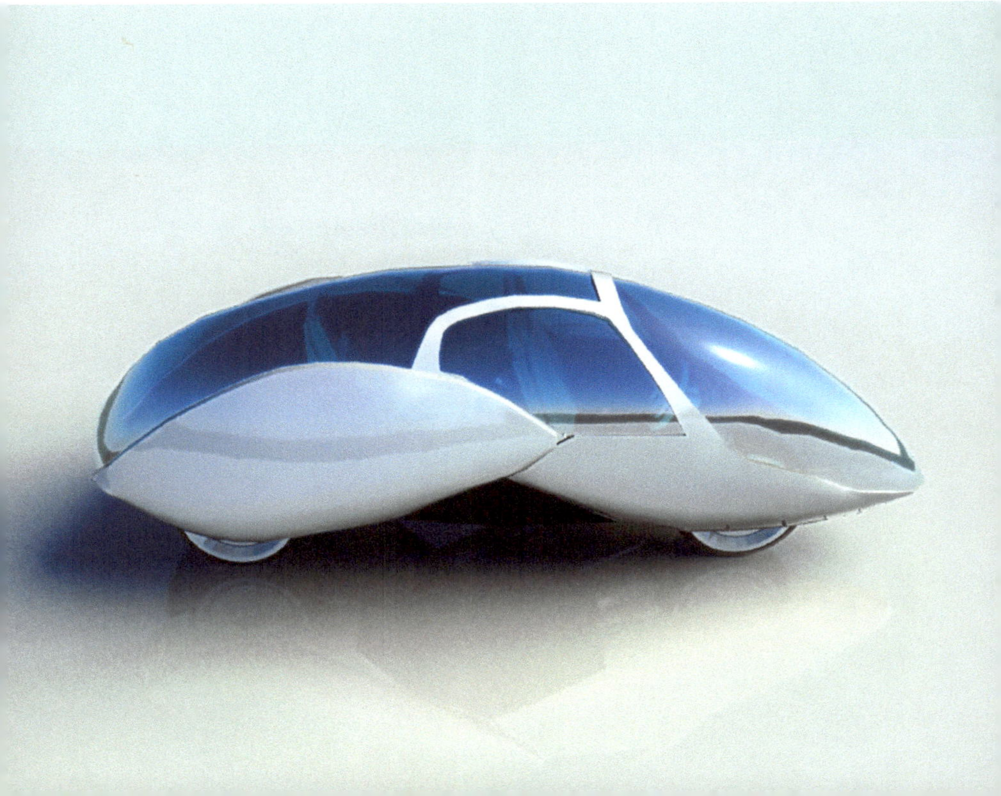

66

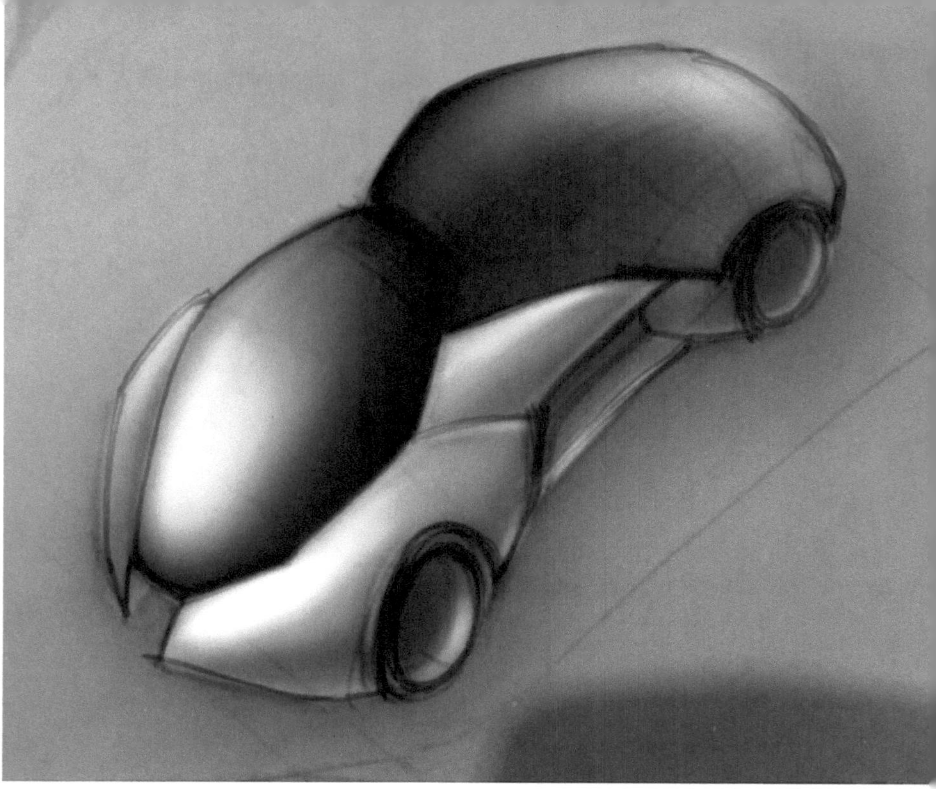

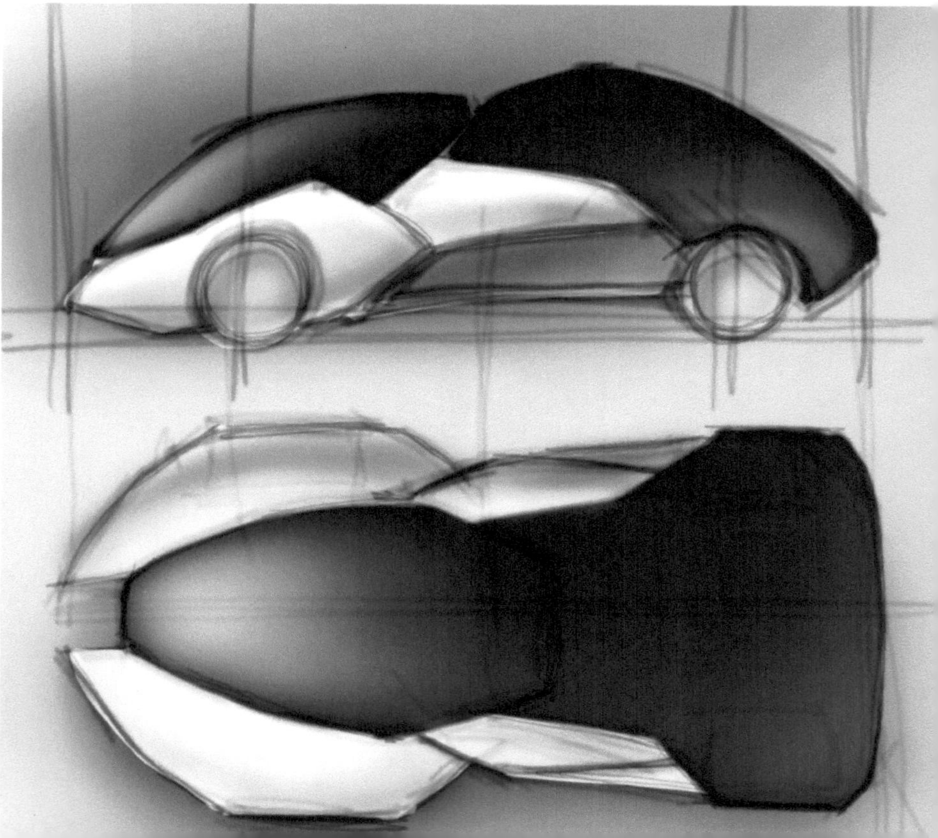

ORIAS

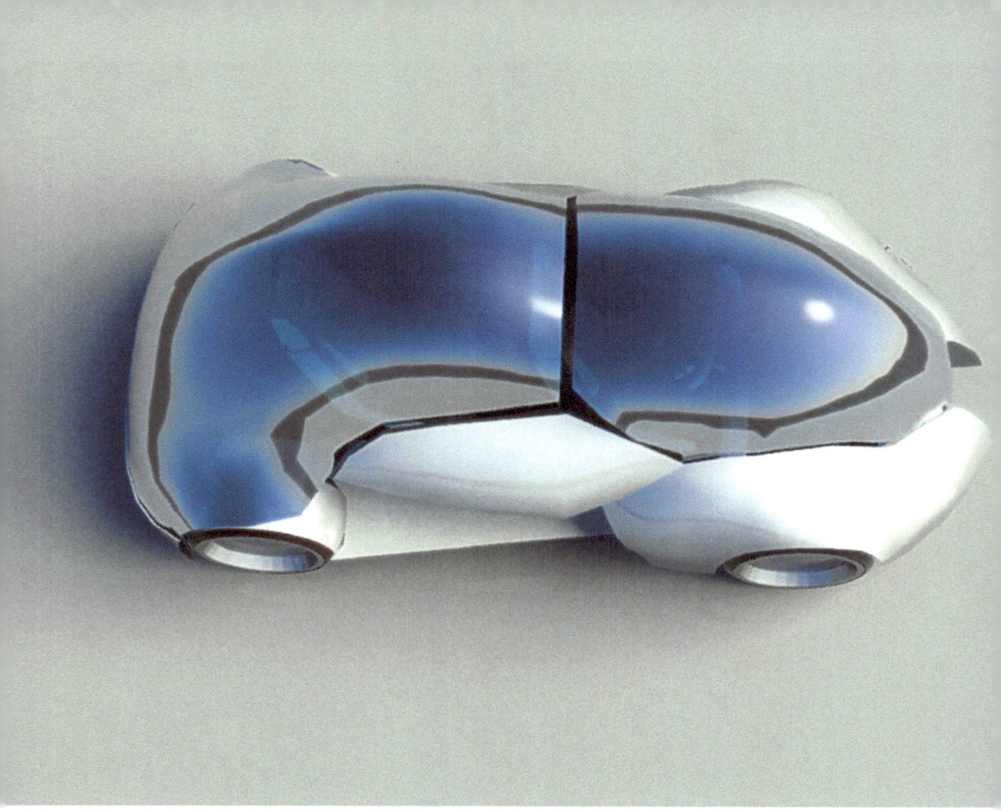

69

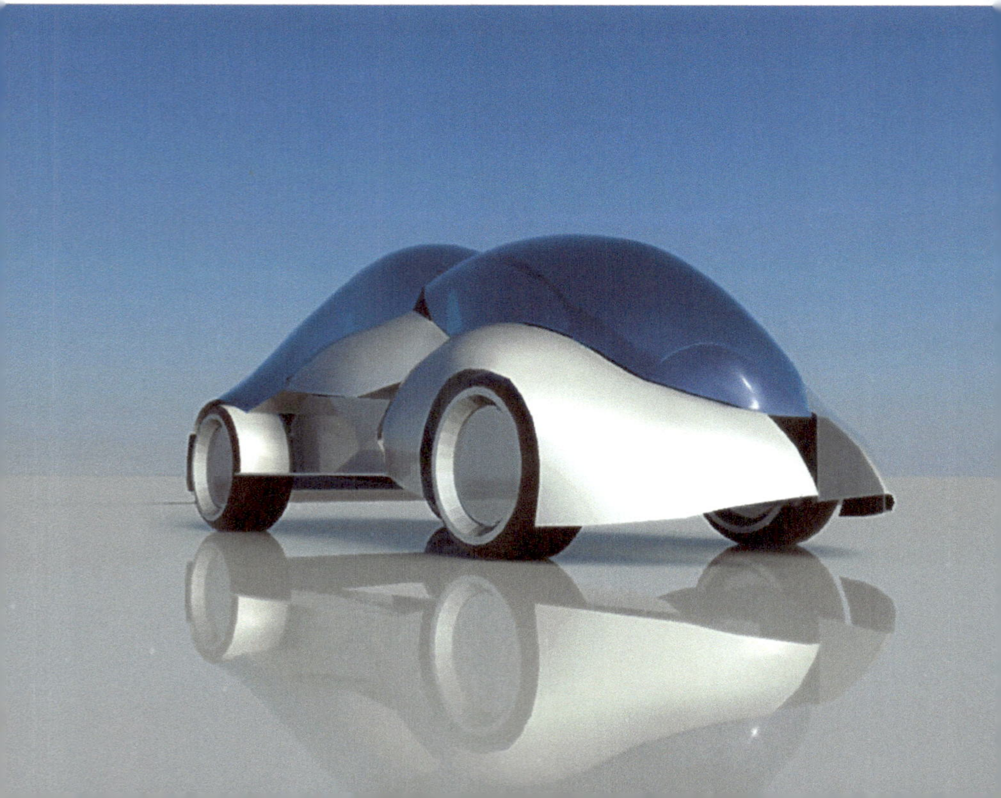

71

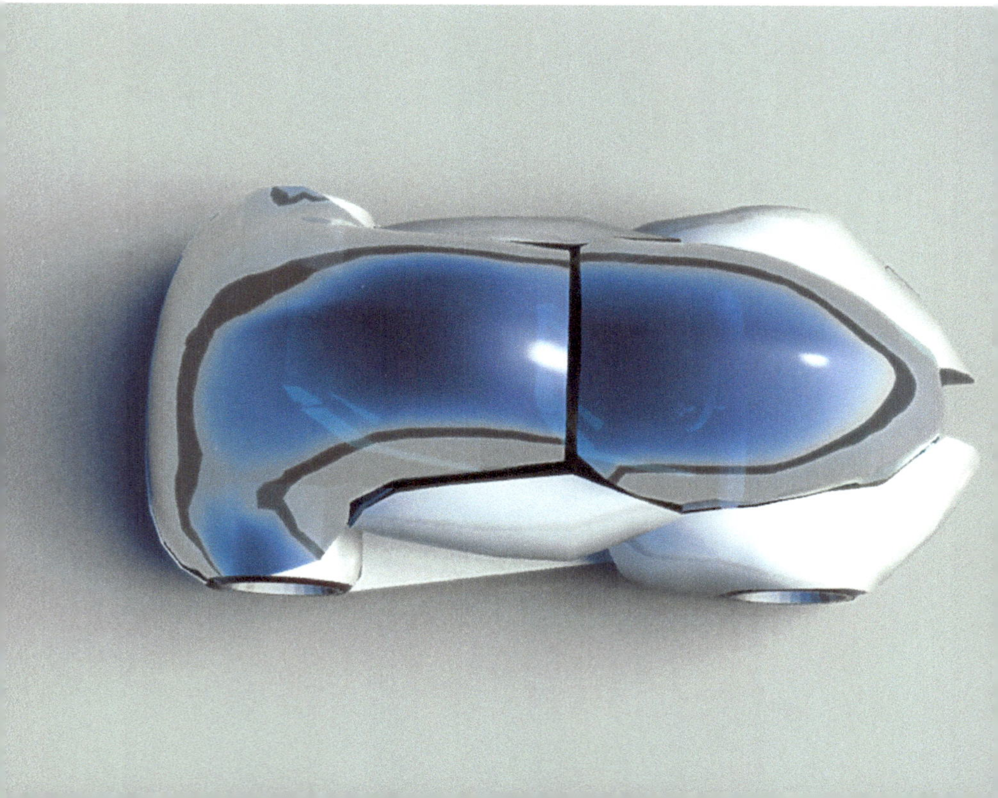

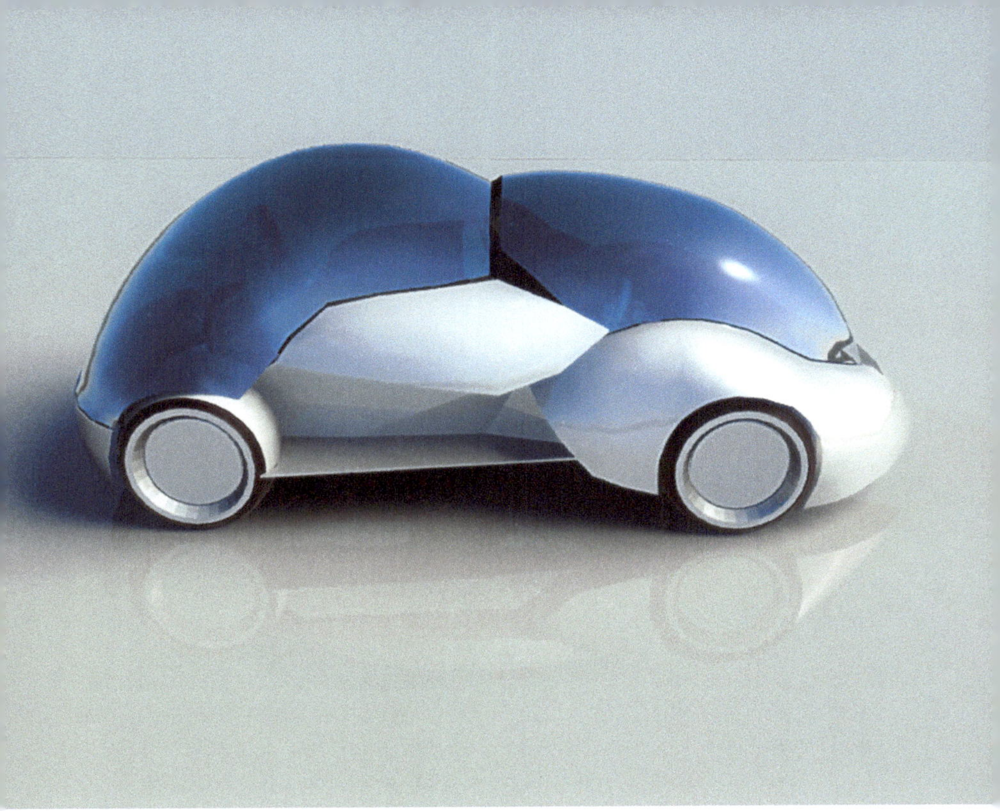

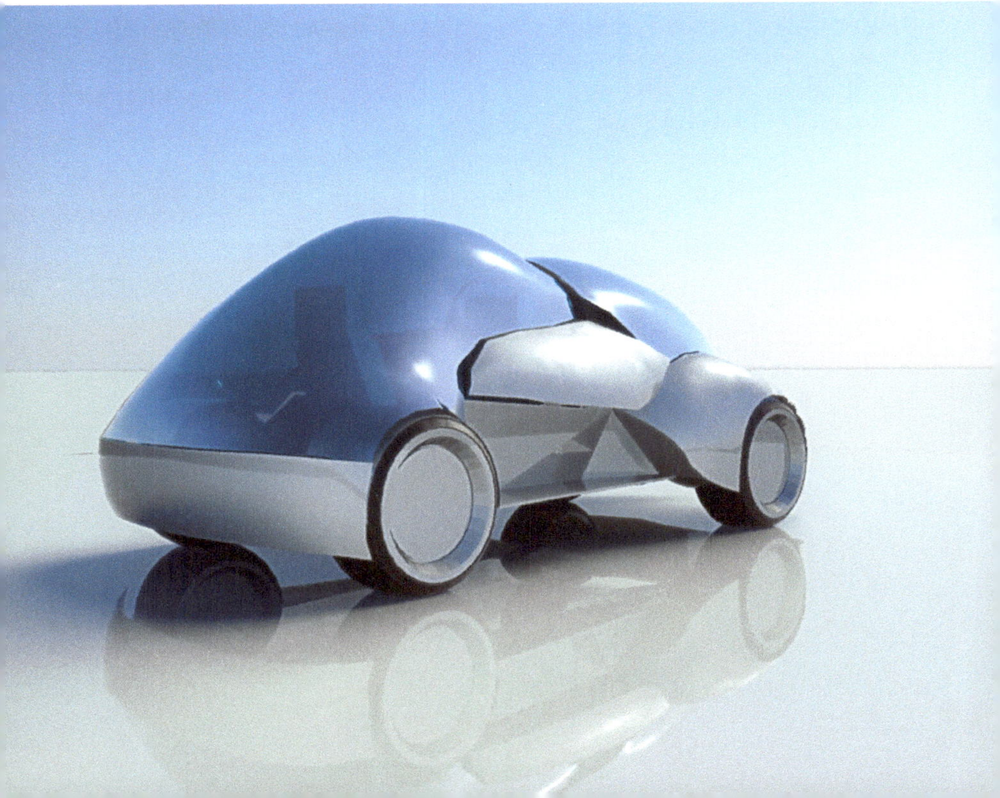

The blood of the dragon nurture millions of silver wombs
in their raging echoes his fury emerges
The charioteer commands over the roaring thunder,
his strikes are guided by the will of his new master
Their wings were sacrifice under the blacksmith forge
His unheard agony moves a wheeled altar

About the ancient combustion engine and the uprising of a
new era where people can live thousands of years in a
month, they move nearly as 107,200 km per hour without
abandon their beds. We were granted with a precious blue
chariot with 6,378.01 km of radius that spin around a
golden star.

ABOUT THE AUTHOR

www.marcoaureliogalan.blogspot.com

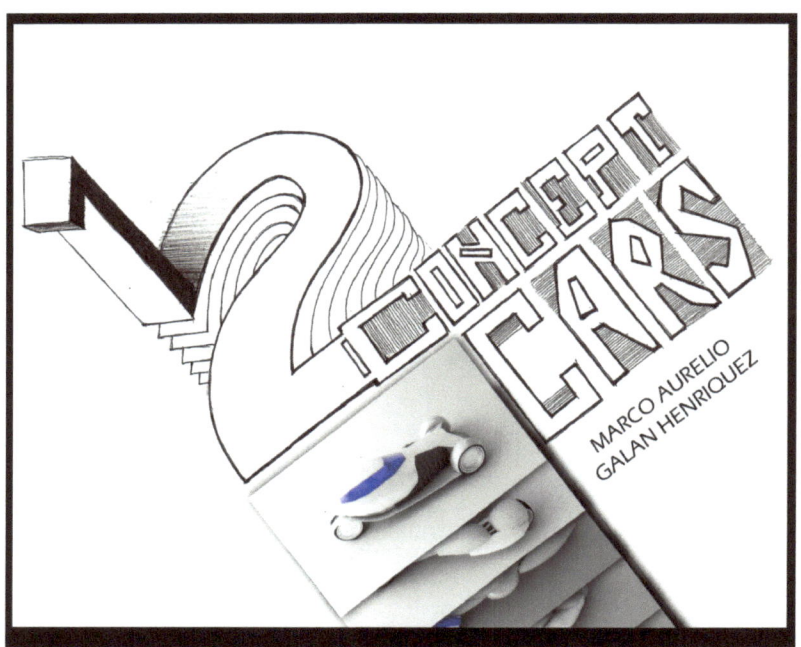

https://www.createspace.com/3671533

12 CONCEPT CARS

EGYPTIAN PANTHEON
A GRAPHIC JOURNEY THROUGH
ANCIENT GODS

https://www.createspace.com/3711902

DESIGN STAGE 1

MARCO AURELIO GALAN HENRIQUEZ

https://www.createspace.com/3777840

Art gallery by Eliana Paola Gomez (Cover)

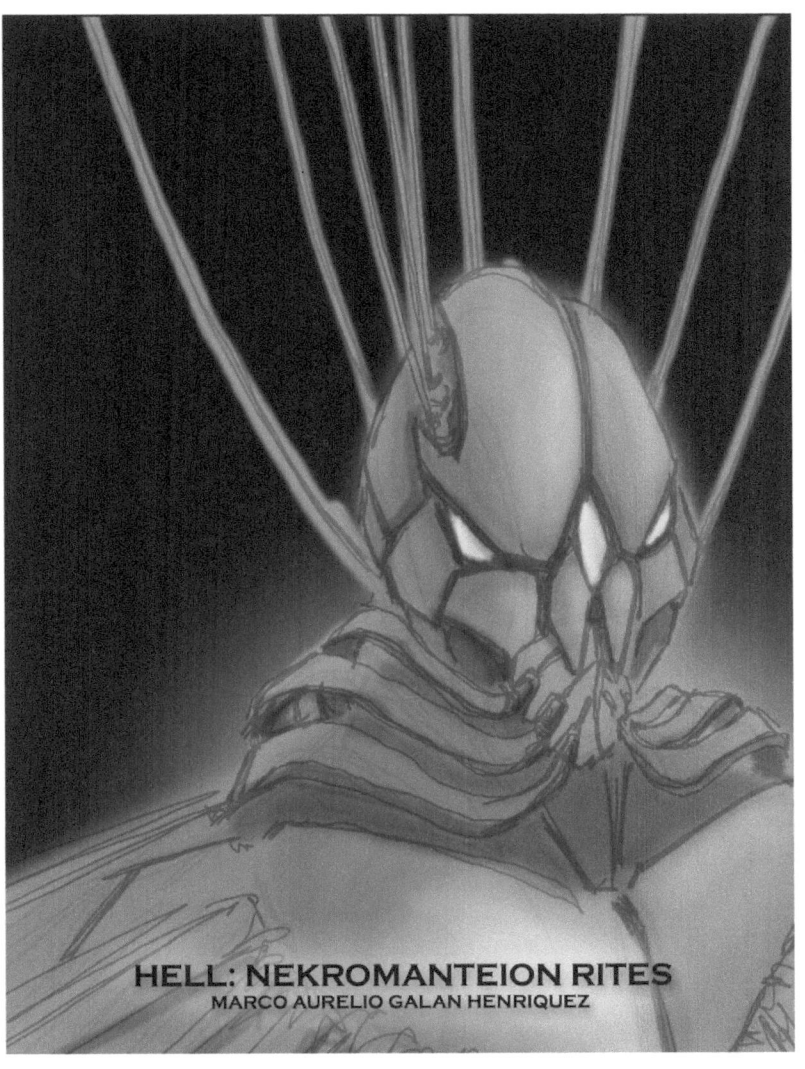

HELL: NEKROMANTEION RITES
MARCO AURELIO GALAN HENRIQUEZ

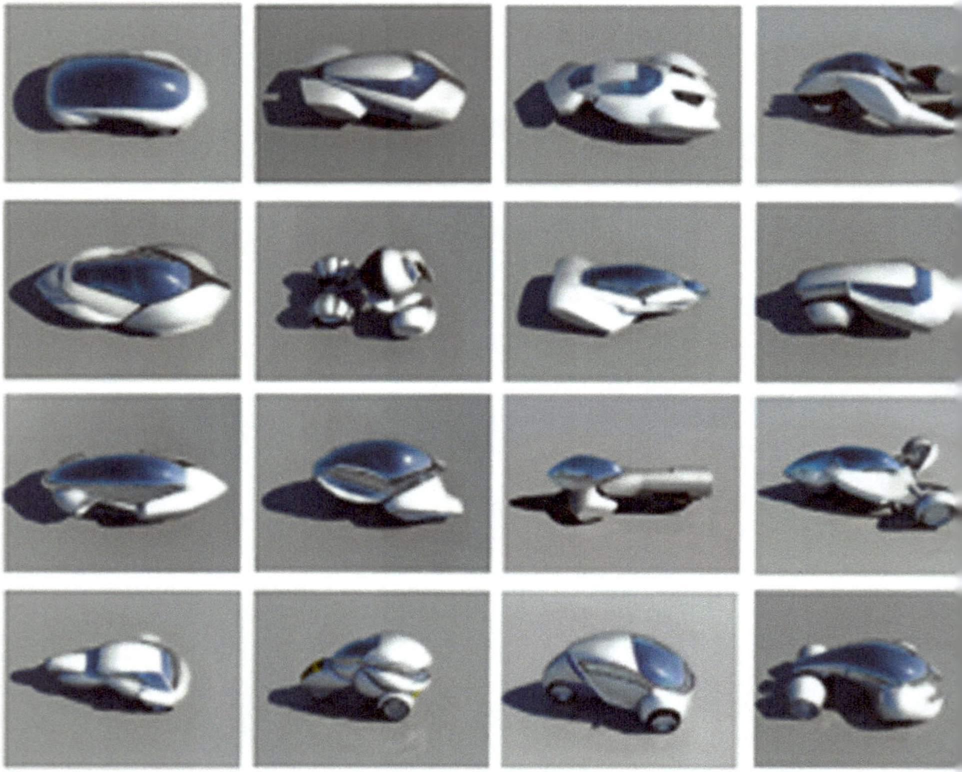

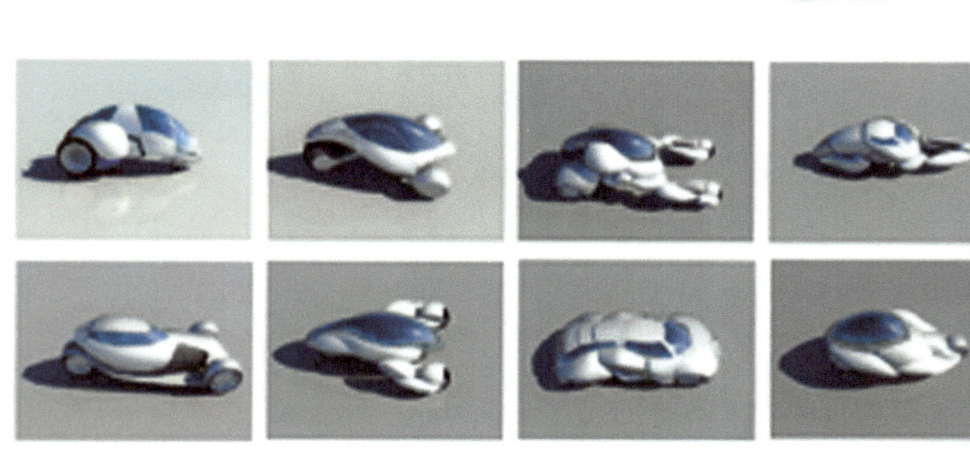

24 BIONIC CARS

MARCO AURELIO GALAN HENRIQUEZ

https://www.createspace.com/3942876

AÑO 2112 V1.0
MARCO AURELIO GALAN HENRIQUEZ

https://www.createspace.com/4245049